READINGS ON

MACBETH

OTHER TITLES IN THE GREENHAVEN PRESS
LITERARY COMPANION SERIES:

AMERICAN AUTHORS

Maya Angelou
Stephen Crane
Emily Dickinson
William Faulkner
F. Scott Fitzgerald
Nathaniel Hawthorne
Ernest Hemingway
Herman Melville
Arthur Miller
Eugene O'Neill
Edgar Allan Poe
John Steinbeck
Mark Twain
Thornton Wilder

AMERICAN LITERATURE

The Adventures of
  Huckleberry Finn
The Adventures of Tom
  Sawyer
The Catcher in the Rye
The Crucible
Death of a Salesman
The Glass Menagerie
The Grapes of Wrath
The Great Gatsby
Of Mice and Men
The Old Man and the Sea
The Pearl
The Scarlet Letter
A Separate Peace

BRITISH AUTHORS

Jane Austen
Joseph Conrad
Charles Dickens

BRITISH LITERATURE

Animal Farm
The Canterbury Tales
Great Expectations
Hamlet
Julius Caesar
Lord of the Flies
Pride and Prejudice
Romeo and Juliet
Shakespeare: The Comedies
Shakespeare: The Histories
Shakespeare: The Sonnets
Shakespeare: The Tragedies
A Tale of Two Cities
Wuthering Heights

WORLD AUTHORS

Fyodor Dostoyevsky
Homer
Sophocles

WORLD LITERATURE

A Doll's House
All Quiet on the Western
  Front
The Diary of a Young Girl

THE GREENHAVEN PRESS
Literary Companion
TO BRITISH LITERATURE

MACBETH

Clarice Swisher, *Book Editor*

David L. Bender, *Publisher*
Bruno Leone, *Executive Editor*
Bonnie Szumski, *Series Editor*

Greenhaven Press, Inc., San Diego, CA

Every effort has been made to trace the owners of copy-righted material. The articles in this volume may have been edited for content, length, and/or reading level. The titles have been changed to enhance the editorial purpose. Those interested in locating the original source will find the complete citation on the first page of each article.

Library of Congress Cataloging-in-Publication Data

Readings on Macbeth / Clarice Swisher, book editor.
    p.   cm. — (The Greenhaven Press literary companion to British literature)
    Includes bibliographical references and index.
    ISBN 1-56510-851-5 (lib. bdg.: alk. paper). —
ISBN 1-56510-850-7 (pbk. : alk. paper)
    1. Shakespeare, William, 1564–1616. Macbeth.
2. Macbeth, King of Scotland, 11th cent.—In literature.
3. Tragedy. I. Swisher, Clarice, 1933–   . II. Series.
PR2823.R37   1999
822.3'3—dc21   98-25242
                                                          CIP

Cover photo: © Hulton Getty/Tony Stone Images

Copyright ©1999 by Greenhaven Press, Inc.
PO Box 289009
San Diego, CA 92198-9009
Printed in the U.S.A.

" *Life's but a walking shadow,*
  a poor player,
That struts and frets his hour
  upon the stage
And then is heard no more. It is
  a tale
Told by an idiot, full of sound
  and fury,
Signifying nothing. **"**

Macbeth, 5.5.24–28

CONTENTS

Chapter 3: Shakespeare's Technique and Craft

Chapter 4: Themes and Structure in *Macbeth*

FOREWORD

*"'Tis the good reader that
makes the good book."*

Ralph Waldo Emerson

The story's bare facts are simple: The captain, an old and scarred seafarer, walks with a peg leg made of whale ivory. He relentlessly drives his crew to hunt the world's oceans for the great white whale that crippled him. After a long search, the ship encounters the whale and a fierce battle ensues. Finally the captain drives his harpoon into the whale, but the harpoon line catches the captain about the neck and drags him to his death.

A simple story, a straightforward plot—yet, since the 1851 publication of Herman Melville's *Moby-Dick*, readers and critics have found many meanings in the struggle between Captain Ahab and the whale. To some, the novel is a cautionary tale that depicts how Ahab's obsession with revenge leads to his insanity and death. Others believe that the whale represents the unknowable secrets of the universe and that Ahab is a tragic hero who dares to challenge fate by attempting to discover this knowledge. Perhaps Melville intended Ahab as a criticism of Americans' tendency to become involved in well-intentioned but irrational causes. Or did Melville model Ahab after himself, letting his fictional character express his anger at what he perceived as a cruel and distant god?

Although literary critics disagree over the meaning of *Moby-Dick*, readers do not need to choose one particular interpretation in order to gain an understanding of Melville's novel. Instead, by examining various analyses, they can gain numerous insights into the issues that lie under the surface of the basic plot. Studying the writings of literary critics can also aid readers in making their own assessments of *Moby-Dick* and other literary works and in developing analytical thinking skills.

The Greenhaven Literary Companion Series was created with these goals in mind. Designed for young adults, this unique anthology series provides an engaging and comprehensive introduction to literary analysis and criticism. The essays included in the Literary Companion Series are chosen for their accessibility to a young adult audience and are expertly edited in consideration of both the reading and comprehension levels of this audience. In addition, each essay is introduced by a concise summation that presents the contributing writer's main themes and insights. Every anthology in the Literary Companion Series contains a varied selection of critical essays that cover a wide time span and express diverse views. Wherever possible, primary sources are represented through excerpts from authors' notebooks, letters, and journals and through contemporary criticism.

Each title in the Literary Companion Series pays careful consideration to the historical context of the particular author or literary work. In-depth biographies and detailed chronologies reveal important aspects of authors' lives and emphasize the historical events and social milieu that influenced their writings. To facilitate further research, every anthology includes primary and secondary source bibliographies of articles and/or books selected for their suitability for young adults. These engaging features make the Greenhaven Literary Companion series ideal for introducing students to literary analysis in the classroom or as a library resource for young adults researching the world's great authors and literature.

Exceptional in its focus on young adults, the Greenhaven Literary Companion Series strives to present literary criticism in a compelling and accessible format. Every title in the series is intended to spark readers' interest in leading American and world authors, to help them broaden their understanding of literature, and to encourage them to formulate their own analyses of the literary works that they read. It is the editors' hope that young adult readers will find these anthologies to be true companions in their study of literature.

INTRODUCTION

The critic Gareth Lloyd Evans has called *Macbeth* Shakespeare's "most haunting play"; Francis Fergusson says it is the "most concentrated of the tragedies." The shortest of Shakespeare's tragedies, *Macbeth* is also his most poetic, and unlike most tragedies, its tragic characters *choose* evil. *Macbeth*'s unusual qualities have given critics a fertile field to till as they analyze its complex techniques and search for its right meaning.

Readings on Macbeth comprises a broad sampling of critical opinion to help readers make sense of this difficult play. Opinions range from the influence of contemporary historical events to conflicting views on the play's structure to the significance of the Porter and the Witches. Contributors include many distinguished Shakespearean critics, such as Lily B. Campbell, G. Wilson Knight, Maynard Mack, and Stephen Booth.

Readings on Macbeth includes many special features that make research and literary criticism accessible and understandable. An annotated table of contents lets readers quickly preview the contents of individual essays. A chronology features a list of significant events in Shakespeare's life placed in a broader historical context. The bibliography includes books on Shakespeare's time and additional critical sources suitable for further research.

Each essay has aids for clear understanding. Individual introductions serve to explain the main points, which are then identified within the essays. Footnotes explain uncommon references and define unfamiliar words. Taken together, these aids make the Greenhaven Press Literary Companion Series an indispensable research tool.

WILLIAM SHAKESPEARE:
A BIOGRAPHY

By today's standards, factual information about William Shakespeare is meager indeed; no diaries, journals, or letters survive to help biographers ascertain the author's personality or his opinions or feelings. Diligent scholars have, however, located institutional records to identify Shakespeare's place of birth and upbringing and the essential events in his family life. They have unearthed records identifying some of his employment history and economic holdings. To supplement the record, scholars have turned to the text of his works and knowledge of Elizabethan history and beliefs to understand Shakespeare the man. Not surprisingly, interpretations differ. As critic Harry Levin observes: "We are less acquainted with what went into his work than what came out of it."

BIRTH AND FAMILY

William Shakespeare was born in Stratford (today called Stratford-upon-Avon) in Warwickshire, a county in the heart of England, on April 23 or 24, 1564. His birth date is presumed from the record of his baptism in Holy Trinity, the Stratford Church of England, on April 26; because many children died in infancy, baptism usually occurred within two or three days of a child's birth. Shakespeare's mother, Mary Arden, came from an old county family. More genteel and prosperous than the Shakespeares, the Ardens provided their daughter with a dowry of land and money, which advanced the status of her husband, John Shakespeare, when the couple married in 1557. John Shakespeare was a glove maker; a trader in wool, timber, and barley; and, for a time, a prominent community leader and officeholder. He began public service as the town ale taster in 1557 and subsequently performed the offices of burgess, constable, town treasurer, alderman, and bailiff, or mayor. In the early 1580s, however, John Shakespeare's financial troubles led to the loss of both his wealth and his governing positions.

William was the third of eight children born to Mary and John Shakespeare. Two daughters—Joan, christened in September 1558, and Margaret, christened in December 1662—died young. Four siblings were born after William reached adulthood: Gilbert, christened in October 1566; a second Joan, christened in 1569; Richard, christened in March 1573 or 1574; and Edmund, christened in 1580. Another daughter, Anne, died at age eight.

EDUCATION

Though no school records exist, Shakespeare likely attended regular English schools like the ones children throughout England attended. Typically, young children first spent a year in an elementary school studying arithmetic and catechism (a summary of the basic principles of Christianity in question-and-answer form) and learning to read and write in English. After age seven, Shakespeare probably attended grammar school at King's New School, where he received rigorous training in Latin. Latin classes were taught by Oxford graduates who often had advanced degrees.

Students were expected to be in their seats by six A.M. in the summer and seven A.M. in the winter for a school day that began and ended with Bible readings, psalm singing, and prayers. Students were drilled in grammar, logic, rhetoric, composition, public speaking, and literature—all in Latin. The curriculum included the Roman dramatists Seneca, Terence, and Plautus; Renaissance religious texts; the Roman poets Horace, Virgil, and Ovid; the complete works of Dutch Renaissance scholar Erasmus; and the works of Roman orators, philosophers, and historians. Shakespeare, who drew from Ovid's *Metamorphoses* for his own plays and poems, likely remembered this classic from his grammar school days. Years later, playwright Ben Jonson disparagingly called Shakespeare's learning "small Latin and less Greek," but this opinion is disputed by biographer Dennis Kay, who writes in *Shakespeare: His Life, Work and Era:* "To argue, as some do, that a man of Shakespeare's background could not have been sufficiently learned to write the works attributed to him, is to fly in the face of the evidence."

Shakespeare's education extended well beyond the Stratford grammar school. Elizabethan law required regular attendance in the Protestant Church of England, so Shakespeare would have grown up listening to readings from the Bible and the *Book of Common Prayer*, the liturgical book of the Church of England. Scholars have counted in Shake-speare's plays allusions to forty books of the Bible and many references to the commandments, quotations from the Psalms, and lines from the prayer book. In *Shakespeare the Man,* biographer A.L. Rowse calls Shakespeare a man educated in "the university of life." His plays display detailed knowledge of the entertainment, social mores, and culture of his native Warwickshire. Price says that we may

> be sure that the knowledge of hawking, hunting, and archery, of horses, dogs, and wild things, of peddlers, shepherds, and farm folk—this store of information in his plays and poems was not acquired only from books, but indicates a normal freedom to roam the countryside and enjoy himself.

Though he lived far from London, Shakespeare had at least a few opportunities to experience some of its cultural riches while a boy in Stratford. When John Shakespeare was bailiff, probably in 1569, troupes of players began to perform in the Guild Hall in Stratford and continued to stage plays every year from the time William was five years old. Though there are no records of John Shakespeare's attendance, as a bailiff he would surely have brought his family to the entertainments. In 1575, Shakespeare had another taste of London life when Queen Elizabeth I visited the earl of Leicester at his castle at Kenilworth, a few miles from Stratford. Called a progress, the queen's entourage included courtiers on horseback, coaches, hundreds of servants, and numerous carts hauling supplies. County crowds gathered to watch the procession go by and perhaps hear a word from the queen. During the queen's stay—for nearly a month—crowds surrounded the castle to watch the pageants, water shows, and fireworks displays prepared in the queen's honor. Shakespeare alludes to entertainments like these in *A Midsummer Night's Dream* and *Twelfth Night,* perhaps recalling the spectacles he saw as a boy.

EARLY MANHOOD

Though no record confirms this, Shakespeare left school at about age sixteen. When he was eighteen years old, he married Anne Hathaway, eight years older than he. Biographers have made much of the evidence that banns for the marriage were called only once, on December 1, 1582, rather than the usual three times; the inference is that church officials hurried the marriage because Anne was already pregnant. However, because Elizabethan custom considered betrothal (engagement) a binding agreement and in some instances the same as marriage, her pregnancy was less unusual than modern customs might consider it.

After the marriage, the couple lived with Shakespeare's family on Henley Street in Stratford. On May 26, 1583, their child Susanna was baptized; twenty months later the young couple had twins, baptized Hamnet and Judith on February 2, 1585. Aside from the facts of his marriage and children, little is known about the way he spent his days. Kay speculates:

> He may have traveled, worked as a schoolmaster, a soldier, or a lawyer, trained as an actor, embraced (or left) the Roman Church, poached deer, or indulged in bouts of heavy drinking. Whatever he did, he found some way of passing the time between leaving school in the late 1570s and springing into action—and celebrity—on the professional stage in London at some time in the late 1580s.

According to one of the myths surrounding Shakespeare's life, he was caught poaching deer in a park belonging to Sir Thomas Lucy of Cherlecote, near Stratford. Historian Nicholas Rowe speculates that Shakespeare might have left his business and family and taken refuge in London to avoid prosecution.

FIRST YEARS IN LONDON

The years 1585 to 1592 are called the "lost years" because no records of any kind document Shakespeare's movements or activities during the period. He probably went to London sometime between 1585 and 1587, possibly joining up with a company of traveling actors or striking out alone on foot. By one route, a man could walk to London in four days if he made twenty-five miles a day, and he could have lodged at inns along the way for a penny a night. In *Shakespeare: A Compact Documentary Life*, Samuel Schoenbaum describes London as Shakespeare would have found it:

> The great city of contrasts spawned stately mansions and slum tenements, gardens and midden-heaped lanes. With the Court close to hand, it was the vital nerve-center for the professions, trade, and commerce, and the arts; London nourished the English Renaissance. Only in the metropolis could a playwright of genius forge a career for himself.

Violent and spectacular entertainments were popular among Londoners of all classes: acrobatic shows and tumbling stunts, bear and bull baiting, and public executions at which crowds were spattered with blood when the headsman's ax severed the head from the shoulders. Historian Roland Mushat Frye states, "The theatres were in daily competition with these bloody sports. It is small wonder that the stage plays tended so much to violent action."

Attending plays, however, was the most popular form of entertainment for all classes, from poor student to aristocrats. Plays were first performed in courtyards of inns, but by the time Shakespeare arrived, London had several theaters. The first, built in 1576 by James Burbage, was called simply the Theatre, and the Fortune, the Swan, the Curtain, and the Rose followed. The theatres consisted of an open stage surrounded by uncovered space where a standing crowd viewed the performance. Three levels of covered seats enclosed the open space. Each theater maintained an all-male resident company of actors performing plays and competing with all the other theaters for popular approval. Female parts were played by boys usually recruited from the boys' choirs in the cathedrals. (Not until 1660 did a woman act onstage.) During the twelve days of Christmas, the companies performed plays in Queen Elizabeth's court to entertain royal guests; throughout the year, traveling troupes drawn from the companies also performed plays in towns and cities outside London.

One story goes that Shakespeare began his career by holding patrons' horses outside the theater; another says that he began as a prompter's attendant. He may have held both jobs for a short time and then advanced to acting before becoming the company's writer. Kay acknowledges that "we are no nearer knowing how and when Shakespeare began writing plays, nor do we know how he acquired the skills and experience to fit him for his profession." Price suggests that Shakespeare's choice of acting as a career must have grieved the hearts of his parents because Elizabethan society looked on actors as riffraff, men of questionable reputation at best. Though attending plays was popular London entertainment, many moralists complained that the jokes were too bawdy and that young men neglected their church duties in favor of playgoing.

THE EMERGENCE OF A PLAYWRIGHT

Shakespeare, an outsider in London, a country man lacking the sophistication and easy manners of Cambridge and Oxford University men, studied the ways of a gentleman, found a mentor, and read widely. Shakespeare looked to Cambridge-educated playwright Christopher Marlowe, who was the same age but who preceded Shakespeare in skillfully combining drama with poetry. Shakespeare studied three successful plays staged in the late 1580s: Thomas Kyd's *Spanish Tragedy* and Marlowe's *Tamburlaine* and *The Jew of Malta*. He emulated romantic elements and imitated the poetic techniques of the works of two British poets: Sir Philip Sidney's sonnets and *The Arcadia*, a prose romance, and Edmund Spenser's *The Faerie Queene*, an allegorical poem glorifying the queen. Moreover, Shakespeare, who loved his country and her history, read the *Chronicles*, published in 1577 and reissued in 1587 by Raphael Holinshed, a historian who came to London early in Elizabeth's reign. Holinshed borrowed from an earlier historian, Edward Halle, whose *Chronicles* also recounted the history of England, especially its royal families. There were no copyright laws in effect in the sixteenth century, so writers were free to borrow from and paraphrase the works of other writers. Shakespeare depended on Holinshed's *Chronicles* most heavily as the source for the history plays, but he also drew on Halle and other sources.

Records show that Shakespeare had already made his mark as a playwright by 1592. *The Tragedy of Titus Andronicus*, Shakespeare's first tragedy, was the first play to appear in 1594 in printed form, but without the author's name. Shakespeare reflected England's political debate of the 1590s concerning the wars with France in, *1, 2,* and *3 Henry VI*. He structured the plot of *The Comedy of Errors* according to a popular school text, Plautus's *Menaechmi*. And *Richard III*, a history with one star player, the callous villain King Richard, anticipated *Macbeth*. The popularity of these early plays elicited a comment in a journal left by Robert Greene, a popular Cambridge-educated playwright. In his *Groatsworth of Wit*, Greene, complaining that the professional actors had forsaken university men like him, specifically attacked Shakespeare:

> Yes trust them not: for there is an upstart Crow, beautified with our feathers, that with his *Tygers hart wrapt in a Players hyde*,[1] supposes he is as well able to bombast out a blanke verse as the best of you: and beeing an absolute *Johannes fac totum*,[2] is in his owne conceit the onely Shake-scene in a countrey.

After Greene's death in 1592, his literary executor, Henry Chettle, issued a printed apology, saying "I am as sorry as if the original fault had been my fault. . . . Besides, divers of worship have reported his [Shakespeare's] uprightness of dealing, which argues his honesty, and his facetious grace in writing, that approves his art."

1. a play on Shakespeare's line from *3 Henry VI*, "O tiger's heart wrapt in a woman's hide!" 2. a "Jack do-everything," a jack of all trades

SHAKESPEARE AS A POET

About the time Greene's comment appeared, plague spread through London, lasting through 1593, and the lord mayor ordered the theaters closed in the interest of public health. Without theater work, Shakespeare made his first appeal to the reading public. He had wanted to be a poet, which he considered a noble occupation; acting and writing plays, he thought, were merely means to support a family. On April 18, 1593, the printer Richard Field obtained license to publish Shakespeare's lengthy poem *Venus and Adonis,* about the passion of the goddess of love, and on May 9, 1594, license to publish another poem, *The Rape of Lucrece,* about the moral dilemma of a chaste Roman wife who commits suicide to escape the shame of having been raped by Tarquin. Shakespeare proofread the copy and monitored the publication of both poems. The typesetter, who selected characters from the type case and placed them as he read the handwritten copy to be reproduced in print, was the only individual ensuring accuracy of the type; if he misread the manuscript, errors appeared in the publication.

Shakespeare also wrote a series of 154 sonnets, which celebrate a beautiful young man and express powerful passion for a mysterious dark lady at whose hands the poet suffers greatly. Since neither the young man nor the dark lady is named, critics have gone to great lengths to verify their identity. Most critics conclude that the twenty sonnets dedicated to the young man and the many others that celebrate him in glowing terms refer to the earl of Southampton, who had become Shakespeare's patron. No less critical energy has been devoted to determining whether or not the sonnets are autobiographical. Most critics concur that they are not, but biographer A.L. Rowse, who thinks they are, agrees that the young man is the earl of Southampton and identifies the dark lady as Emilia Bassano, daughter of an Italian musician in the queen's court.

THE TURNING POINT IN SHAKESPEARE'S CAREER

In 1594 Shakespeare turned away from sonnet writing and established himself with an acting company since, with the end of the plague, the theaters reopened and the earl of Southampton's patronage ended. By the summer of 1594, a group of actors formerly with other companies had been assembled under the patronage of Henry Lord Hunsdon, lord chamberlain to the queen, calling themselves Lord Chamberlain's Men. They played at various theaters, including the Theatre, the Curtain, and the Swan. Among the company's permanent members were Henry Condell, John Heminge, Shakespeare, Richard Burbage (son of the Theatre's builder, James Burbage), William Sly, and Will Kempe. Burbage, the famous tragedian, and Kempe, the famous comedian, played leading roles in plays Shakespeare wrote specifically for their talents. From then on, Shakespeare was completely involved in the theater: He wrote for the company, acted in the plays, shared in the profits, and eventually became an owner. While in London, he worked hard and played little; he lived during those years as a lodger in quiet rooms near the playhouses where he could write without interruption.

Shakespeare's major early successes came between 1593 and 1598. *Love's Labour's Lost,* probably the only play without a borrowed plot, portrays contemporary social and political life. It was published in 1598, the first identifying him by name as the author. Critics have called it and *The Two Gentlemen from Verona* lyrical because both contain passages of beautiful description and passionate feelings. Shakespeare's style in these early comedies shows evidence of the influence of playwright John Lyly, whose adaptions from Greek mythology are written in euphuistic style, an artificial style rich in repartee and word play, musical lyrics, and elaborate imagery. With *A Midsummer Night's Dream,* Shakespeare had already surpassed Lyly in inventiveness of plot and characters from the fairy world. *The Taming of the Shrew* and *The Tragedy of Romeo and Juliet* exemplify other characteristics of his early plays—intricate plots and long explanatory speeches written in stiff verse.

Shakespeare also wrote history plays about England's past kings: *Richard II, 1* and *2 Henry IV, Henry V,* and *King John.* After the early *Richard III,* Shakespeare realized that the War of the Roses had originated in the reign of Richard II, and wrote the later play about the earlier king. The two parts of *Henry IV* portray the undoing of Henry IV (Henry Bolingbroke) and the preparation of his son Hal to become Henry V. *King John,* described by scholars as puzzling and uneven, depicts the political crises of an early-thirteenth-century king.

1 and *2 Henry IV* were particularly popular with the audiences, who loved the humor of the fat knight Falstaff. Falstaff's unrestrained indulgence in sensual pleasures, his love of telling big lies, and his own laziness are set against great good humor and consistent wit. Sidney Lee says, "Shakespeare's purely comic power culminated in Falstaff; he may be claimed as the most humorous figure in literature." After

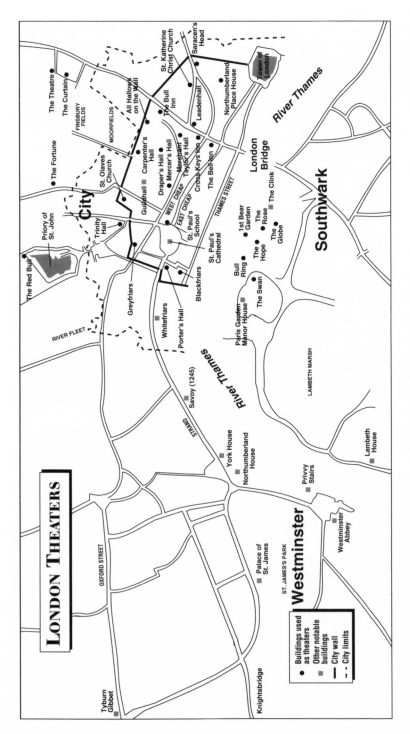

Falstaff disappeared as a character in the history plays, Queen Elizabeth requested that Shakespeare write another in which Falstaff falls in love. Shakespeare complied with *The Merry Wives of Windsor*, but in this play Falstaff is the butt, not the creator, of humor. During this period, Shakespeare also wrote the comedies *Much Ado About Nothing*, and *The Merchant of Venice*, both of which have two stories or two threads of interest. Shakespeare received wide praise for his early works. Among the most notable were comments by Francis Meres, a learned Cambridge graduate, who in *Palladis Tamia: Wit's Treasury* called Shakespeare the greatest man of letters:

So the sweet witty soul of Ovid lives in mellifluous and honey-tongued Shakespeare, witness his *Venus and Adonis*, his *Lucrece*, his sugared *Sonnets* among his private friends, etc.

As Plautus and Seneca are accounted the best for Comedy and Tragedy among the Latins: so Shakespeare among the English is the most excellent in both kinds for the stage. . . .

As Epius Stolo said, that the Muses would speak with Plautus tongue if they would speak Latin: so I say that the Muses would speak with Shakespeare's fine filed phrase, if they would speak English.

Ben Jonson, who criticized Shakespeare's learning, also praised him, calling him the "Soul of the age! / The applause, delight, and wonder of our stage, . . . not of an age, but for all time." Shakespeare was called witty and gentle, qualities reflected by antiquarian and gossip John Aubrey, who writes: "He was a handsome, well-shap't man: very good company, and of a very readie and pleasant smoothe Witt."

IMPORTANT PERSONAL EVENTS

Despite his growing fame, Stratford was still the center of Shakespeare's personal life. In 1596 and 1597, Shakespeare was occupied with three significant family matters. First, in August 1596, Shakespeare returned to Stratford when Hamnet died. With the death of his eleven-year-old son, died Shakespeare's hope of perpetuating the family in his name, as Anne Shakespeare was forty and could not be expected to have another child. Shakespeare expressed his grief in the play he was writing at the time, *King John*:

Grief filles the room up of my absent child,
Lies in his bed, walks up and down with me,
Puts on his pretty looks, repeats his words,
Remembers me of all his gracious parts,
Stuffs out his vacant garments with his form.

(3.4)

Second, though he had no son to carry on the family name, Shakespeare pressed to obtain the title and coat of arms of a gentleman, a status evidently important to him. Shakespeare applied and paid cash for a grant in the name of his father. On October 20, 1596, Garter King of Arms William Dethick issued a coat of arms with a falcon and a silver spear and declared Shakespeare a gentleman by birth. The family evidently felt themselves entitled to the honor, for they chose as their motto the phrase *Non sanz droict* (Not without right). Finally, in May 1597, Shakespeare purchased New Place, a large home in the center of Stratford with two barns and two orchards and gardens. Before he was thirty-five years old, Shakespeare had achieved the status of gentleman, property owner, and playwright, but he had lost his only male heir.

THE NEW GLOBE

In 1597, James Burbage, who had built the Theatre in 1576, died, and the Lord Chamberlain's Men lost their lease. About the same time, Puritans increased their opposition to what they perceived as the immorality of the city theaters. To circumvent Puritan criticism, the Lord Chamberlain's Men found backing to dismantle the Theatre, move the boards across the Thames from London's city center, and rebuild the theater, which they renamed the Globe. By this time, Shakespeare had acquired enough wealth to buy a one-tenth share in the new theater.

The Globe outshone its competitors; it held two thousand spectators and was equipped with a bigger stage, a cellerage for graves and ghosts, a curtained space for intimate and surprise scenes, and a balcony. The audience was closer to the players, and the players had more flexibility to move quickly from scene to scene. *Henry V*, in which Shakespeare played the part of the chorus, anticipates the Globe. In the prologue, he refers to the new theater with excitement.

> A kingdom for a stage, princes to act
> And monarchs to behold the swelling scene! . . .
>   Can this cockpit[3] hold
> The vasty fields of France? Or may we cram
> Within this wooden O[4] the very casques[5]
> That did affright the air at Agincourt?[6]

In the epilogue Shakespeare displays his characteristically

3. playhouse 4. playhouse 5. the actual helmets 6. the French village where Henry V defeated a larger French army

humble attitude toward himself, writing,

> Thus far, with rough and all-unable pen,
> Our bending[7] author hath pursued the story,
> In little room[8] confining mighty men,
> Mangling by starts[9] the full course of their glory.

Though he himself may have been self-assured, he speaks as a humble gentleman throughout his works, self-deprecatingly calling himself "a worthless boat," "inferior far" to Marlowe. Others found this attitude charming, and Shakespeare gained a reputation for congeniality.

OUTPOURING OF COMEDIES AND TRAGEDIES

After 1598, Shakespeare's comedies and tragedies appeared quickly one after another. He turned from English history to Roman history and used *Lives*, by Greek philosopher and biographer Plutarch, as a source for plots. *The Tragedy of Julius Caesar*, dated 1599, explores Brutus's character and motives. In addition, Shakespeare wrote three comedies suited to Will Kempe's talents. Besides *The Merry Wives of Windsor*, Kempe starred in *As You Like It* and *Twelfth Night*, whose title comes from its performance before the queen during Twelfth Night of 1599–1600.

After 1600, Shakespeare wrote his greatest tragedies, distinguished from the earlier works by more subtle language and deeper spirit. *Hamlet* and *Othello* came first. Shakespearean scholar and critic G.B. Harrison says that "*Hamlet* is in every way the most interesting play ever written"; for nearly four hundred years, it has challenged actors and scholars to interpret Hamlet's character. *Othello*, a unified and focused play, portrays evil in the character of Iago as he exploits Othello's jealousy and Desdemona's innocence to destroy them and their love.

The opening of the Globe marked a new phase in Shakespeare's reputation and art. Firmly established as the leading dramatist in London, his plays became more refined and subtle. Price says, "Art has replaced artifice. The style has become so fully expressive of the thought that audiences and readers are unconscious of the poet's devices." Shakespeare was interested in the workings of the human psyche, and objectively reveals his characters' minds in their actions and speeches. The soliloquies of Brutus, Hamlet, and Iago, for example, lay bare their intentions and their very souls.

---

7. bowing 8. theater 9. marring the story by telling it in fragments

Among his friends and fellow playwrights, Shakespeare had a reputation for writing headlong with little attention to revision. Aubrey reports playwright Ben Jonson's opinion of Shakespeare's method of writing: "He was wont to say that he never blotted out a line in his life. Sayd Ben Johnson, I wish he had blotted out a thousand." In the annual Shakespeare Lecture of the British Academy in 1972, M.M. Mahood acknowledges faults in the texts. Mahood says, "Shakespeare's plays abound in loose ends, false starts, confusions, and anomalies of every kind." Many examples can be found in the comedies; for instance in *The Taming of the Shrew,* the characters Sly and the Hostess disappear from the play.

Though Shakespeare continued to write, the period from 1598 to 1604 brought significant personal diversions. In September 1601, his father died in Stratford. The following May, Shakespeare bought 107 acres of farmland in Old Stratford for £320, and in September a cottage on Walkers Street. On March 24, 1603, Queen Elizabeth, who had actively supported Lord Chamberlain's Men, died. James I succeeded her, took over the company, renamed it the King's Men, and supported the players even more avidly than the queen had, making them an official part of the court, doubled their salaries, and increased their annual court appearances from three to thirteen. In addition, he gave them license to perform in any town or university. These changes required Shakespeare to pay greater attention to the approval of two audiences, the court and the Globe. Shakespeare's increase in income allowed him to invest £440 in tithes in parishes in Stratford and surrounding towns, investments that brought additional income of £60 a year.

THE KING'S MEN

From 1604 to 1608, as a member of the King's Men, Shakespeare's art changed again. He wrote two transitional comedies in which he experimented with techniques to work out dramatic problems. *All's Well That Ends Well,* an uneven play seldom performed, involves a young woman who tricks a man into becoming her husband. *Measure for Measure,* called a problem play because the plot poorly fits the theme, concerns a woman who compromises her chastity to save her brother.

After 1604, Shakespeare's tragedies probed even more deeply into the minds of their heroes. *The Tragedy of King Lear* was first performed in King James's court during the

Christmas holidays of 1606. Critics regard *Lear* as Shakespeare's greatest play, though not his most popular. The play has a double plot; Lear suffers at the hands of his daughters and Gloucester at the hands of his son. Both die, but each has one child who remains loyal. The play's greatness lies in the psychological depth of Lear's character and the stark reality of both human nature and nature's elements.

Shakespeare wrote *Macbeth* in 1606, as a tribute to James I on the occasion of a state visit from the king of Denmark. The play is set in Scotland, James's home before he became king of England. The good character Banquo is a member of the Scottish Stuart family, an ancestor of James. Shakespeare also honored the king, who was interested in witchcraft, by incorporating the three Witches into the play. Though he did not find King James an honorable man, Shakespeare fulfilled his duty to the king upon whose patronage he depended. Like *Lear, Macbeth* reaches below the rational level into the subconscious, where primitive experiences lie in recesses of the mind; the tragic Macbeth and Lady Macbeth, having plotted the murder of Duncan to put Macbeth on the throne, see their plot undone and suffer mental anguish before they too die.

After the four great tragedies, Shakespeare returned to Plutarch's *Lives* as a source for three more. *The Tragedy of Antony and Cleopatra* picks up the story of Roman history where *Julius Caesar* left off. *The Tragedy of Coriolanus* is a political play in which Shakespeare exposes the weakness of all manner of politicians and presents the crowd in a tone more bitter than his exposé of the crowd in *Julius Caesar*. *Timon of Athens*, an unfinished play, tells about an ancient Greek mentioned briefly in Plutarch's *Lives*.

During this period when Shakespeare wrote one or more plays a year and kept a busy schedule of productions at court and at the Globe, a few facts are know about his personal life. His daughter Susanna married a well-known medical doctor from Stratford named John Hall on June 5, 1607. In September 1608, his mother, Mary Arden Shakespeare, died, and in October 1608, Shakespeare was named godfather to the son of Stratford alderman Henry Walker, whose son was named William in honor of Shakespeare.

In 1609 a respected publisher, Thomas Thorpe, published without Shakespeare's knowledge a book entitled *Shakespeare's Sonnets: Never Before Imprinted*. Without copyright laws in existence, any person with a manuscript in hand could register it, publish it, and become its owner. Two factors indicate that Shakespeare had no part in the publication: The dedication appearing under the title was by the publisher, a common practice when an author was not involved; and the volume contained numerous errors and even missing words, unlike the editions of the two poems that Shakespeare had prepared for printing. After Thorpe's edition, the sonnets were not reprinted until 1640; some scholars think a displeased Shakespeare took measures in 1609 to prevent further circulation.

THE FINAL PERIOD

After the outpouring of tragedies, Shakespeare used changes in theater ownership and attendance to create a new kind of dramatic art. Blackfriars, a private theater owned by Richard Burbage, had been leased to a boys' company. Burbage, Shakespeare, and other actors bought back the lease and began performances there for upper-class audiences more like those at court. Blackfriars audiences liked new plays, while the public audiences at the Globe preferred old favorites. This situation suited Shakespeare, whose new plays for Blackfriars were neither comedies nor tragedies. Some critics have called them romances; others, tragi-comedies. These plays express themes of reunion after long separation followed by reconciliation and forgiveness. The plots revolve around children lost and then found, divided parents brought together, or an innocent person threatened but rescued. Before characters find a haven, they have been through storms and stress, encountered evil, or endured suffering. Rowse says: "For all their happy endings, these plays have an atmosphere full of suggestion and symbol, suffused with tears."

Shakespeare wrote four plays in this new form. *Pericles* is a transitional play, portions of which appear to have been written by a second playwright. After experimenting with *Pericles*, Shakespeare wrote *Cymbeline*, probably in 1610, a melodrama about an innocent girl who flees mistreatment and encounters a host of crises before she is reunited with her repentant husband. *The Winter's Tale*, written in 1610 or 1611, is a moving tale of wrongs committed by one generation and reconciled in the children.

The Tempest, a play written for James I to celebrate a court wedding, is Shakespeare's farewell to the theater. This fairy tale about a magician and his beautiful daughter ends with the reconciliation of two generations. G.B. Harrison praises *The Tempest:*

Shakespeare has finally achieved complete mastery over words in the blank-verse form. This power is shown throughout the play, but particularly in some of Prospero's great speeches, . . . or in his farewell to his art. There is in these speeches a kind of organ note not hitherto heard. Shakespeare's thought was as deep as in his tragedies, but now he was able to express each thought with perfect meaning and its own proper harmony.

Prospero, the magician of *The Tempest*, recounts his tricks in words that some critics think apply aptly to Shakespeare. After cataloging the marvels he has conjured up over the years, from raging storms to corpses rising from the grave to a dimmed sun, he announces "this rough magic / I here abjure. . . . I'll break my staff, / Bury it certain fathoms in the earth, / And . . . I'll drown my book." Shakespeare's only play after this farewell was *Henry VIII*, a series of historical episodes full of pageantry, music, and ceremony. During the June 29, 1613, performance of *Henry VIII*, a spark from a cannon set the thatch roof of the Globe alight and the building burned to the ground. Though the Globe was rebuilt in 1614, there is reason to believe that the players' books and many of Shakespeare's original manuscripts were lost in the fire.

From 1612 on, Shakespeare divided his time between Stratford and London, and once went to Parliament to lobby for better roads between the two cities. In 1612 his brother Gilbert died, followed by his brother Richard the next year. Shakespeare spent 1614 and 1615 in Stratford enjoying his retirement and his daughters, but information about his wife, Anne, seems to be nonexistent. The parish register of Holy Trinity shows that on February 10, 1616, Shakespeare's younger daughter Judith was married to Thomas Quiney, the son of Shakespeare's old friend Richard Quiney. On March 25, 1616, while he was in fine health, Shakespeare made a will. He left a dowry and additional money to Judith and all lands and houses to his older daughter Susanna and her heirs. He left his wife to the care of his daughters and willed her the next-best bed, perhaps reasoning that Susanna and her husband needed the bigger, better one. To his sister, he left money for clothes and the home on Henley Street. He gave small amounts of money to friends and money for rings to fellow actors of the King's Men, and he left money for the poor in Stratford. A month later, after a trip to London, he suddenly became ill and died on April 23, 1616, at fifty-two. As he lay dying, the chapel bell knelled for the man for whom love was the center of the universe and the central subject of his many works.

THE FIRST FOLIO

During his lifetime, Shakespeare made no effort to publish his works, other than the two long poems. His plays belonged to the members of the theater company, who sold individual plays for publication when readers requested them in the early 1600s. In 1623—the year Anne Hathaway Shakespeare died—two actors from the King's Men, Henry Condell and John Heminge, collected Shakespeare's plays and published them in what is known as the First Folio, and they have been in print ever since. In their introduction Condell and Heminge appealed to readers "from the most able, to him that can but spell. Read him, therefore, and again, and again. And if then you do not like him, surely you are in some manifest danger not to understand him."

Some skeptics, doubting Shakespeare's genius and education, have speculated that someone else wrote the plays. Doubts appeared as early as 1694 and recurred in 1785, when Francis Bacon was identified as a probable author; James Spedding, Bacon's editor and biographer, however, dismisses the notion: "I doubt whether there are five lines together to be found in Bacon which could be mistaken for Shakespeare, or five lines in Shakespeare which could be mistaken for Bacon." In 1921 Thomas Looney theorized in *Shakespeare Identified* that Edward de Vere, seventeenth earl of Oxford, was the true Shakespeare, basing his research on the correspondences between de Vere's travels, education, and social class and details in the plays. Most reputable critics believe that such theories are advanced by the uninformed. As Price says: "No first-rate scholar has ever accepted the evidence offered by the Baconians or others who argue that Shakespeare did not write the dramas that his fellow-actors, Heminge and Condell, published as his."

CHAPTER 1

Macbeth:
Historical
Context

READINGS ON
MACBETH

The Historical Context of *Macbeth*

Garry Wills

Garry Wills cites many productions of *Macbeth* that have failed, often because acts 4 and 5 lag; heavily cut adaptations have been more successful. Wills argues that both complete productions and adaptations ignore important historical information that gives the play a context; specifically, references to publicity surrounding the Gunpowder Plot to blow up Parliament in 1605. Highlighting those references, which recur in *Macbeth*, gives purpose and vitality to the late problem acts. Garry Wills has taught at Johns Hopkins University. He was invited to deliver the annual Oxford University Press Lectures at the New York City Public Library in 1993. He is the author of *Chesterton: Man and Mask*, and *Explaining America: The Federalist*, and editor of *Values Americans Live By.*

If *Macbeth* is such a great tragedy, why do performances of it so often fail? Its unhappy stage history has created a legendary curse on the drama. Superstitious actors try to evade the curse by circumlocution, using "the Scottish play" at rehearsals to avoid naming it, *Macbeth*. Even great actors and actresses— John Gielgud and Glenda Jackson, to name just two—have been unable to make the play work. Some have hesitated to direct the play, or refused roles in it, from a knowledge of its dismal record. Adaptations of it can be more successful than the original—Verdi's opera, Kurosawa's movie (*Throne of Blood*), Orson Welles's abbreviated film phantasmagoria.

THE CURSE ON *MACBETH*

Just what is the curse on *Macbeth*? Anecdotes accumulate about mishaps in the staging. But accidents plague all forms of theater. Heavy scenery is moved hastily in cramped and ill-lit spaces. Actors fight careful but risky duels, often half-blinded by spotlights or atmospheric murk. Sniffles are passed around in the confluence of backstage, onstage, and auditorium airs, variously cooled or heated (or both at the same time). Actors get laryngitis; stand-ins forget stage business and confuse their fellows. Cues are mistaken. Props break.

Since many people, from stage technicians to financial backers, spend their whole careers in the theater, they are bound to die at some time—and no one notices what play they were connected with at the moment. But when Lilian Baylis, the legendary manager of the Old Vic Theatre in the 1930s, died, her troupe was putting on *Macbeth*, so people talked of the curse. Laurence Olivier twisted his ankle on the opening night of his 1955 *Macbeth* and had to restrain the leaps essential to his interpretation. But he injured himself in several other plays, notably *Coriolanus*, and nobody called *those* plays cursed.

The inevitable problems of any production have taken on special menace with *Macbeth* because actor after actor is frustrated by the seeming unplayability of the piece. Elizabeth Nielsen claimed: "No actor since Shakespeare's time seems to have made a name for himself playing the part of Macbeth." Kenneth Tynan agreed: "Nobody has ever succeeded as Macbeth." By critical consensus there seems to have been only one entirely successful modern performance of the play, Olivier's in 1955. And even Olivier had failed to bring the play off in his first attempt (done in 1938, the "cursed" Lilian Baylis production).

OLIVIER'S 1955 SUCCESS

Where failure is so common, it is important to see why the exception worked. Reviewers were disappointed, in 1955, during the play's opening scenes, usually the most successful. Olivier seemed to lack some of his normal energy—his patented kinetic jolt—in the "surefire" encounter with the witches, or in the scenes before and after Duncan's murder. This is precisely where Macbeth and his wife fuel each other's resolution in some of the most intense exchanges Shakespeare ever wrote.

But Olivier began to soar in the banquet scene, where the Macbeth of most productions starts falling apart. Olivier's Macbeth, who made his low-intensity first choices of evil in a hesitating way, rouses himself to accept his fate heroically. Instead of cringing before the ghost's repeated apparition, Olivier manned himself to leap on the banquet table and run at the ghost, sword drawn, in an exaltation of defiance. Some crazed enlargement of this Macbeth makes him grow toward his doom, climaxed with the frenzied duel that ends the play.

However one judges Olivier's interpretation of the play as a whole, he had identified its real problem, the way it sputters toward anticlimax in most presentations of Acts Four and Five. Macbeth and his wife, whose interchanges are the best parts of most productions, are never seen together in those final acts. His wife, in fact, is seen only once, in the brief (but effective) sleepwalking scene. The play seems to dissipate its pent-in tensions as it wanders off to England, brings in new characters (Lady Macduff and her child, Hecate and her train), deals at tedious length with the question of genuine Scottish heirs, and substitutes the pallid moral struggle of Malcolm with Macduff for the crackling interplay of Macbeth and his Lady.

Even Olivier did not make most of these later scenes interesting in themselves. But people sat through them with a sense of purpose, waiting to see what new mad heights Macbeth would reach in his climb toward heroic criminality. Olivier solved the play's problem by turning Macbeth into Tamburlaine.[1] It was a very Marlovian reading of Shakespeare. It had the advantage of keeping the hero alive outside the claustrophobic whispering scenes of the first act. Better a cosmic hero than a closet drama. Even Tamburlaine is preferable to Raskolnikov.[2] Actors like Gielgud or Paul Scofield turned the first half of the play into *Crime and Punishment*, and then had nowhere to go with the second half.

ADAPTATIONS OF *MACBETH* SUCCEED

This explains why the adaptations of *Macbeth* succeed, in our time, better than the original play. They cut away or cut down all the inert stuff toward the end. Verdi's opera spends less time on both the final acts than on Act One alone (the murder of Duncan). Verdi excised the Lady Macduff scene, Malcolm's testing of Macduff, the dealings with the English

---

1. In Marlowe's play the ambitious Tamburlaine continues his defiance and rebellion to the end. He rebels against the king of Persia, defeats the heir to the Crown, defeats and taunts the Turkish emperor, captures Damascus, and attacks Babylon. In the end he is dragged in a chariot and dies. 2. The main character in Fyodor Dostoeyvsky's novel *Crime and Punishment*

court (with its king who heals by touching), and the Siwards (father and son). Kurosawa and Welles observe roughly the same proportion between a lingered-on first half of the play and a drastically reduced second half. The effect of thus "frontloading" *Macbeth* is to shear away any larger social context for the protagonists' strugglings. Verdi was explicit about the intimacy he desired for the Macbeths, even in the extrovert form of opera. He chose to do the opera when he did because he lacked the singers for a larger dramatic ensemble. None of his music dramas has so much sung whispering, to be done in a "hollow" voice (*voce cupa*). The whole play is absorbed, so far as possible, into Macbeth's inner state—as it is in Welles's film, where surreal stones and caves are projections of his own anfractuous mental scenery. [As critic D.J. Snider said:] "The inner truth is that these [witches'] shapes are himself—his own desires, his own ambition." Inner truth—mainly Macbeth's but also his wife's—is what many people want or expect from the play. "Outer truths" fall away; they distract when they do not detract from the inner quest.

The result is a lopsided play, dead in the most embarrassing places, toward the end, where the action should accelerate and the interest be intensified. A frontloaded play is a back-crippled play. That is the real curse. Olivier overcame this structural defect by a personal tour de force. He wrenched the audience's attention out of its old patterns, redistributing the emphases, achieving equilibrium by making the first scenes less absorbing than they can be. He made the "crippled" part of the play scramble and skip, overcoming its inertia with his own prodigious energies, harbored for this late explosion. When that individual feat is removed, all the faults of the play remain.

MACBETH IN HISTORICAL AND DRAMATIC CONTEXT

But are they faults? I shall adopt, as a working hypothesis, . . . the view that Shakespeare was not a bungler, that he did not fill the second half of his play with matter of no interest to his audience. How might one test that hypothesis? One way would be to look at the other dramas being put on at the same time as *Macbeth* (roughly, in 1606 or the 1606–1607 Christmas–New Year's season). If they contained similar material, we can assume that the material had some theatrical appeal, no matter how difficult that may be for us to understand. It is a separate question whether that appeal

MACBETH AS A GUNPOWDER PLAY

In this excerpt from Witches and Jesuits, *Garry Wills describes King James I's efforts to control the attitude of the public toward the Gunpowder Plot.*

Godfearing English subjects interpreted the attempt on their sovereign's life and government in 1605, when a religious cold war existed between England and papal Rome. A cell of papists—the "enemy within" of that time, directed from Rome by skulking Jesuits—had trundled keg after keg of gunpowder into a vault under Parliament. A munitions expert named Guy Fawkes was discovered with the detonating materials, ready to ignite the fuse (train). . . .

The King disseminated his official version of the Plot in a flood of religious propaganda. . . . James intended his reading of the Plot to become central to England's sense of identity. That is why he kept up a long campaign of indoctrination, to inculcate the lessons of the Plot as a statement of his kingdom's place in God's providence. The national character was at stake in the way the Plot was described and the delivery from it celebrated. The long history of Guy Fawkes Day festivities shows how successful the King was in this project. . . .

Issuing after and around the official statements, both popular and learned literature dwelt on the Plot and its discovery. Censorship of books and plays normally discouraged acrid theological and political controversy; but this ban was relaxed after the Powder Treason, to channel public wrath into approved directions.

---

can be revived today. The first thing is to ask what effects Shakespeare was aiming at for his own audience.

Later civilizations might wonder why twentieth-century Americans were so interested in frontier mercenaries of the preceding century—in "gunfighters." If people in that future world could know only one or two westerns, this odd taste might be dismissed as anomalous. But if they were to discover that dozens of westerns were made together, the films' shared traits would help bring into focus what people considered appealing in the genre. This would not explain the variations that make great art of common plots—what separates, say, a classic movie like *The Searchers* from the latest item off the assembly line of Roy Rogers films. But no one could doubt, with the range of westerns being produced, that the figure of the gunfighter had great symbolic importance to mid-twentieth-century Americans.

So let us take the scene that most disconcerts modern actors and directors in *Macbeth*—Act Four, Scene Three, with the stylized long intellectual game by which Malcolm tests Macduff's willingness to compromise with evil. If we should find similar scenes in other plays being put on at the same time, we might conclude that they held a particular interest for those attending plays in 1606. We do find such plays, and in all of them there is an interest in the uses of deception to test loyalty, and in words as equivocal in their meaning.

The witches' cauldron scene, the necromancy,[3] also embarrasses critics—by its length among other things, which encourages editors and directors to delete the Hecate speeches and songs of the First Folio. But what if we found necromancy scenes of a very similar sort in other plays of 1606? I shall argue that we do. And here is the most interesting aspect of this test: the same plays that have the equivocal-word tests also have the necromancy scenes. A *cluster* of common elements is beginning to emerge. This might seem odd or implausible if these elements were not parts of a larger similarity, in which they are naturally incorporated. *All these plays have reference to the Gunpowder Plot of 1605,*[4] the overriding matter of political interest in the succeeding year, prompting sermons, treatises, ballads, pamphlets, and satires, as well as plays. All this literature shared common images and language.

If we were to see "sneak attack" used over and over in 1942, no matter what the context, we would recognize that those hearing the words could not help but connect them somehow with the 1941 raid on Pearl Harbor. In the same way, when we see words like "vault" and "train" (noun) and "mine" (verb) repeatedly used in the literature (in and outside the theater) of 1606, we have to catch echoes of those words' canonical use to describe what the Powder Plotters tried to do—blow up the entire government of England. The event and its aftermath—the trials of the Plotters, the rites set up to commemorate their dis-

---

3. The practice of supposedly communicating with spirits in order to predict the future. 4. The Gunpowder Plot was a plan to blow up Westminster Palace while King James I, the royal family, the House of Lords, and the House of Commons were assembled there for the opening of Parliament. Angered by James's harsh laws against Catholics, five Catholic men dug a tunnel from an adjacent house to the palace and placed thirty casks of gunpowder directly under the meeting place. Because of leaks, the plot was discovered. On November 4, 1606, agents entered the cellar, found Guy Fawkes, a conspirator, there with the gunpowder and arrested him. Fawkes, other conspirators, and priests were executed in January 1606. England still celebrates November 5 as Guy Fawkes Day with bonfires, fireworks, and effigies of Fawkes carried through the streets.

covery and capture, the elaboration of an official interpretation of all the surrounding circumstances—established the atmosphere in which people attended the theater in 1606 (just as surely as Pearl Harbor established the atmosphere in which people attended movies in 1942 and 1943). There was a rash of Gunpowder plays in 1606.

MACBETH AS A GUNPOWDER PLAY

What makes a Gunpowder play? References to the Plot are one essential. These references must be obvious, although indirect (the condition of even relaxed censors' rules). But some larger themes are also essential. The typical Gunpowder play deals with the apocalyptic destruction of a kingdom (attempted or accomplished), with convulsions brought about by secret "mining" (undermining), plots, and equivocation. And witches are active in this process. When that pattern occurs, along with direct references to the Powder Treason, one has a Gunpowder play. The pattern occurs in *Macbeth,* as well as in these contemporary dramas:

John Marston, *Sophonisba*

Thomas Dekker, *The Whore of Babylon*

Barnabe Barnes, *The Devil's Charter*

There are many other plays, earlier or later, that deal with some of these themes—with witchcraft, equivocation, political apocalypse, tested loyalties, secret plots. Aspects of those plays will be looked at, where they are relevant; but they do not have the particular constellation of all these factors, presented at the time of the Plot and in the language of the Plot.

Macbeth looks like a different play when we consider it in this context, in conjunction with these other artifacts. That does not of itself make it a better play. John Ford's *The Searchers* is not a great movie because of what it shares with western "serials" or B movies. But at least we know, from the collocation with other westerns, what *kind* of movie *The Searchers* is. By historical accident, we have forgotten what kind of play *Macbeth* is; and before deciding how good it is of that kind, we must recover the kind. That will involve, at the outset, recovering the way the Gunpowder Plot filled and colored the popular imagination in its immediate aftermath.

This new context is bound to affect the way we judge modern productions of the play. A focus on the larger social drama of the Gunpowder Plot makes for a drama less exclusively centered on Macbeth and his wife—which means one less confined to the earlier parts of the drama. It is interesting to note that the idea of a "curse" on the play arose only after the Hecate scenes in the last half were excised. No one thought the play cursed when David Garrick acted in it during the eighteenth century, or Edmund Kean in the nineteenth. Admittedly, the text used then was "unauthentic" in ways that went beyond the Hecate scenes. But those adaptations (unlike the modern ones by Welles and Kurosawa) had strong second halfs. The question is: can we recover a view of the play that makes for a strong second half, without resorting to the kinds of additions William Davenant made in the Restoration period? *Macbeth* was once playable. If it could be made playable again, the curse would disappear. We would recognize that the curse grew out of twentieth-century performing practice (based on twentieth-century editing practice), not out of the play itself.

Macbeth's Dramatic Allusions

R.A. Foakes

R.A. Foakes compares *Macbeth* with various traditions of drama and discusses James I and his influence on the play. While Foakes can show that the play fits many theatrical, historical, and critical trends, he repeatedly asserts that *Macbeth* goes beyond them. R.A. Foakes has taught at the University of Kent in England and edited plays for the New Arden Shakespeare series. He is the author of *Shakespeare: From Satire to Celebration.*

In writing *Macbeth*, Shakespeare transformed to his own ends a mode of tragedy that had been long established. The play is basically a tragedy of ambition, in which is enacted the rise to power and subsequent fall of an aspiring prince. Such a description, while oversimple, serves at one and the same time to suggest both the links *Macbeth* has with medieval tragedy and how far Shakespeare moved beyond its limits.

Medieval tragedy was not so crude as the famous definition of Chaucer's Monk would indicate:

Tragedie is to seyn a certeyn storie,
As olde bookes maken us memorie,
Of him that stood in greet prosperitee,
And is yfallen out of heigh degree
Into myserie, and endeth wrecchedly.

The falls of great men were, in fact, treated as Christian moral fables; by showing how Fortune destroys good and bad alike, medieval tragedy encouraged a contempt for the inconstancy of Fortune, as expressed by the Monk in his advice:

Lat no man truste on blynd prosperitee.

The action of Fortune, setting a man up and then casting him down, was a latent theme in those morality plays which

R.A. Foakes, "Introduction," in *The Tragedy of Macbeth*, by William Shakespeare (New York: The Bobbs-Merrill Company, 1968). Reprinted by permission of the author.

showed mankind, or Everyman, reduced to wretchedness before being finally saved by the intervention of Mercy; and this theme became prominent in the sixteenth century as the morality play developed into the secular interlude. In John Skelton's play *Magnificence* (after 1515; printed 1533), the fall of a great prince was still treated allegorically; but later, and especially after the success of *The Mirror for Magistrates* (1559)—a collection of poems recounting the downfall of figures from British history—many plays were written dealing with historical events and people. These plays on historical themes became increasingly concerned with questions of sin, guilt, and retribution, however much the moral might remain, in the words of the Induction to *The Mirror for Magistrates*,

> That when thou seest how lightly they did lose
> Their pomp, their power, and that they thought most sure,
> Thou mayst soon deem no earthly joy may dure.
>
> (lines 117–19)

TRAGEDIES OF AMBITION BECAME SUCCESSFUL

Out of the interplay of these and other developments there came into being, as one mode of tragedy successful on the Elizabethan stage, plays concerned with ambitious princes, and based on real, or what were then thought to be real, historical personages and events. Some of these plays, like Shakespeare's *Henry VI*, portrayed a series of multiple tragedies arising from the miseries of civil wars, and suggest a political rather than a personal thematic interest. Some continued to do little more than show the rise and fall of a character in terms of Fortune's wheel, turning from prosperity to defeat that impels an outcry like Edward IV's

> Though Fortune's malice overthrow my state,
> My mind exceeds the compass of her wheel.
>
> (3 *Henry VI*, IV.iii.46–7)

[Shakespeare's contemporary] Christopher Marlowe, in the first part of *Tamburlaine*, broke the pattern by showing a hero striding to ever greater conquests, apparently immune to Fortune's malice, but Shakespeare's early work suggests that he began with more conventional ideas of the falls of great men, such ideas as Richard II indicates when, in his self-dramatizing way, he imagines

> . . . sad stories of the death of kings,
> How some have been deposed, some slain in war,

Some haunted by the ghosts they have deposed,
Some poisoned by their wives, some sleeping killed,
All murdered. . . .
                                        (*Richard II*, III.ii.156–60)

The theme of the ambitious prince finally overthrown was developed in several of Shakespeare's plays; it is one of the repeated subjects of *Henry VI*, and becomes dominant in *Richard III*. Richard has no concern for Fortune until he is brought low, but he has no conscience either, and as a tragic figure he belongs much more with earlier patterns of tragic development than with Shakespeare's maturity. For, in creating Brutus in *Julius Caesar*, and then Macbeth, Shakespeare went beyond ideas of Fortune and retribution for crimes committed, to exploit further possibilities in the theme of the ambitious prince. He made his central dramatic concern the growing involvement in evil, the self-deceptions, and the mental torture of a naturally good or even pious man succumbing to temptation, trying to justify himself, and being tormented by his conscience. The play of *Macbeth* was the culmination of a long development of tragic writing on the theme of the rise and fall of an ambitious prince, but it transcends all that preceded it in the subtlety and profundity with which the nature of ambition, and its effects on human character, are explored.

THE INFLUENCE OF SENECAN TRAGEDY

Macbeth also belongs to, but transcends, another long and important dramatic tradition, that of Senecan tragedy. [Roman playwright] Seneca's plays had begun to be translated from the Latin in 1559; and their highly melodramatic and rhetorical exploitation of the horrors of murder (often of a wicked tyrant) and its gruesome revenge became the basis of much early Elizabethan tragedy. Kyd's *The Spanish Tragedy* (printed 1592) was extremely popular and influential in establishing the conventions of the Elizabethan revenge tragedy, and Shakespeare had used most of its elements in *Titus Andronicus* (1594) and other early works. The heroes of such plays were often, like Richard III, tyrants and "Machiavels," cruel and practiced in deceit, who fascinated the Elizabethan audience by their lusty delight in their own cunning. The exuberant and indiscriminate sensationalism of the early drama was richly if erratically theatrical, but it was the work of a generation of playwrights to tame, extend, and humanize the conventions they inherited. By the time of *Macbeth* the possibilities of this tradition were being much more fully explored and developed—by Shakespeare in such plays as *Hamlet*, and by many of his contemporaries, including Marston, Tourneur, and Chapman. The villain-hero, the long succession of murders, the use of night, madness, and such supernatural elements as mysterious prophecies, ghosts, and other apparitions—all these are the traditional Senecan and revenge elements imaginatively transmuted into a deeper realization of the motives and horror of Macbeth's actions and of the working out of his doom.

CRITICS SEE *MACBETH*'S COMPLEXITY

Not for a long time did critics of *Macbeth* begin to explore in depth its subtlety and profundity. When critical commentary on *Macbeth*, as on Shakespeare's other plays, began to flourish in the eighteenth century, Macbeth and Lady Macbeth were often seen rather too simply in terms of evil. . . . Then, in 1785, [critic] Thomas Whately made an extended comparison of Macbeth and Richard III in order to show that, unlike Richard, Macbeth's "natural disposition . . . is not bad." This comparison was also used by [essayist William] Hazlitt, who further distinguished Macbeth from Richard; Macbeth is "accessible to pity, is even the dupe of his uxoriousness,[1] and ranks the loss of friends and of his good name among the causes that have made him sick of life." The growing recognition of the complexity of Macbeth as a "character of imagination" is marked in [British poet] S.T. Coleridge's comments on the way in which Macbeth "mistranslates the recoilings and ominous whispers of conscience into prudential and selfish reasonings, and after the deed, the terrors of remorse into fear from external dangers.". . .

The general emphasis of criticism was still on character, and this culminated in the famous analysis of the play by A. C. Bradley in his *Shakespearean Tragedy* (1904). He emphasized the sublimity of the two central figures, proud, peremptory, and fired with a passionate ambition to rule. For Bradley the special characteristic of Macbeth as tragic hero was that "this bold ambitious man of action has, within certain limits, the imagination of a poet," suggesting that his contact with the supernatural, and his intimations of con-

1. excessive submission or devotion to one's wife

science, of moral ideas, come to him through images. In this perception, and in Bradley's sense of the play's atmosphere ("a black night broken by flashes of light and colour"), he pointed the way forward to what was to become a particular concern of much twentieth-century criticism: the poetry, imagery, and symbolism of *Macbeth*. . . .

AN AMBITIOUS MAN WITH A POET'S IMAGINATION
Macbeth's dagger soliloquy in act 2, scene 1 illustrates his imagination.

Is this a dagger which I see before me,
The handle toward my hand? Come, let me clutch thee!
I have thee not, and yet I see thee still.
Art thou not, fatal vision, sensible[1]
To feeling as to sight? or art thou but
A dagger of the mind, a false creation,
Proceeding from the heat-oppressed brain?
I see thee yet, in form as palpable[2]
As this which now I draw.
Thou marshall'st[3] me the way that I was going,
And such an instrument I was to use.
Mine eyes are made the fools o' th' other senses,
Or else worth all the rest. I see thee still;
And on thy blade and dudgeon[4] gouts[5] of blood,
Which was not so before. There's no such thing.
It is the bloody business which informs[6]
Thus to mine eyes. Now o'er the one half-world
Nature seems dead, and wicked dreams abuse
The curtain'd[7] sleep. Now witchcraft celebrates
Pale Hecate's[8] offerings; and wither'd murther,
Alarum'd by his sentinel, the wolf,
Whose howl's his watch,[9] thus with his stealthy pace,
With Tarquin's ravishing strides,[10] towards his design
Moves like a ghost. Thou sure and firm-set earth,
Hear not my steps which way they walk, for fear
Thy very stones prate of my whereabout
And take the present horror[11] from the time,
Which now suits[12] with it. Whiles I threat, he lives;
Words to the heat of deeds too cold breath gives.

1. **sensible:** able to be felt 2. **palpable:** obvious, clear 3. **marshall'st:** conductest 4. **dudgeon:** handle 5. **gouts:** drops 6. **informs:** creates forms 7. **curtain'd:** with the bed curtains drawn 8. **Hecate:** goddess of witchcraft 9. **howl's . . . watch:** who tells the time by howling 10. **Tarquin's . . . strides:** Tarquin, king of Rome, lusted for Lucrece and ravished her. 11. **present horror:** the silence of midnight 12. **suits:** matches

Such criticism has aroused the objection that subtleties of verbal meaning are given an emphasis quite out of proportion to their actual impact on the audience. So it may be argued that few in an audience witnessing *Macbeth* notice the scattered imagery of clothing. Furthermore, such criticism has a tendency to issue in propositions (for example, that the play is a "statement of evil," or that the symbolism of the child is dominant) which the total experience of the action does not support. Criticism which focuses on character is equally liable to give too little weight to the richness of the poetic texture in *Macbeth*, which is, in its language, the most compressed and metaphorical of all the tragedies. Perhaps the main critical problem now is to harmonize the two basic approaches to the play, so that we may come fully to understand how its complexities of language are involved with and contribute to its complexities of character and action.

THE INFLUENCE OF JAMES I

In writing *Macbeth*, Shakespeare turned to Scottish history for his material for the first and only time. His main source for the play was the *Chronicles of Scotland* in Raphael Holinshed's *Chronicles of England, Scotland and Ireland* (1577; issued in a revised and enlarged edition, the one Shakespeare used, in 1587); and out of the stories he found there of the murder of King Duff, the reign of Macbeth, his murder of Banquo and overthrow by Malcolm, Shakespeare fashioned his tragedy. There is little doubt that he was drawn to a Scottish theme by the coming of King James VI of Scotland to London in 1603, when he succeeded Queen Elizabeth I and began his reign as James I of England. . . .

There is nothing to associate *Macbeth* specifically with a court performance, but the text contains plenty of evidence, even beyond its general Scottish theme, to connect it with King James. In the first place, the King was interested in witchcraft. In 1597 he had published a treatise called *Demonology*, in which he affirmed his belief that the Devil makes servants of ignorant or superstitious women, teaches them his arts, and enables them as witches to do all sorts of mischief. Such creatures should be brought to trial, wrote James, and although judges should beware of condemning anyone whose guilt was not certain, all proven witches should be punished with death. "I pray God," the treatise ended, "to purge this country of those devilish practices: for they were never so rife in these parts as they are now.". . .

If witchcraft was a subject that interested King James, so too was the Scottish history on which the play is based. For according to the *Chronicles*, Banquo was James's own ancestor, and the King could scarcely have failed to be stirred by Macbeth's growing certainty that, as he says,

> For Banquo's issue have I filed my mind;
> For them the gracious Duncan have I murdered;
> Put rancours in the vessel of my peace
> Only for them; and mine eternal jewel
> Given to the common enemy of man,
> To make them kings, the seeds of Banquo kings!
>
> (III.i.64–9)

These kings appear finally as apparitions, called forth by the Witches (IV.i.110). The prophecy (I.iii.67) by three "Weird Sisters" that Banquo's successors should "govern the Scottish kingdom by long order of continual descent" was recorded in Holinshed's *Chronicles*. . . .

The play has other connections with King James. Some are matters of minor details, such as the reference in II.iii.9, which is almost certainly to the defense of equivocation by the Jesuit Father Garnet during his trial for treasonable complicity in the Gunpowder Plot of 1605, a defense which had excited James's anger; and the passage about "touching for the King's Evil" (IV.iii.146–59), a power of healing scrofula[2] by laying-on of hands traditionally ascribed to royalty, is a reminder that James prided himself on possessing this power. There is also a more general connection, since James had written with some feeling in his advice to his son, *Basilikon Doron* ("King's Gift" [Edinburgh, 1599; London, 1603]) on the subject of the good king and the tyrant. . . .

What the links with King James show is the way in which the coming of James of Scotland to London turned Shakespeare's thoughts to witchcraft and to Scottish history, and stimulated him to write a great play.

---

2. a form of tuberculosis affecting the lymph nodes, most often found in children

Literary and Political References in *Macbeth*

Maynard Mack

Maynard Mack contrasts the simplicity of Macbeth's story as told in Raphael Holinshed's *Chronicles*, Shakespeare's source, with the complexity of Shakespeare's play. After citing *Macbeth*'s relevance to contemporary issues, Mack identifies the play's resemblance to well-known mythical stories of Satan, Faust, and Adam and Eve, and argues that in the final scenes it takes on elements of an allegory personifying death. Maynard Mack taught English at Yale University, the University of Toronto, and the University of California at Berkeley. He is the author of *King Lear in Our Time*, and *Alexander Pope: A Life*, and editor and contributor to many scholarly volumes.

After *Lear, Macbeth* seems at first glance a simple play. Seen in one light, it simply tells the brutal story of a Scottish usurper whom Shakespeare had read about in one of his favorite source-books, Raphael Holinshed's *Chronicles of England, Scotland, and Ireland.* Holinshed's Macbeth is an arresting figure, not so much because of his murderous career, which seems to have been only a little in excess of the habits of his time, as because he is said during his first ten years of rule to have "set his whole intention to mainteine justice," and during his last seven years to have begun to "shew what he was, instead of equitie practising crueltie."

Shakespeare, though no historian, knew that no man wears a mask of virtue for ten years, only to reveal that he was "really" a butcher all along. This oddity in Holinshed's conception may have challenged him to speculations that ended in a conception of his own: that of an heroic and essentially noble human being who, by visible stages, deteriorates into a butcher. The great crimes of literature, it has been well said, are mostly committed by persons who would ordinarily be thought incapable of performing them like Othello, like Brutus in *Julius Caesar*, like Raskolnikov in Dostoevsky's *Crime and Punishment.* The hero that Shakespeare draws in *Macbeth* is no exception. At the beginning of the play, even the thought of murder stands his hair on end, makes his heart knock at his ribs (1.3.135). By the end, he is too numb to care. His wife's death scarcely stirs him, and the wild cry of her women in their grief only reminds him of what he can no longer feel:

> The time has been my senses would have cooled
> To hear a night-shriek, and my fell of hair
> Would at a dismal treatise rouse and stir
> As life were in't. I have supped full with horrors.
> Direness, familiar to my slaughterous thoughts,
> Cannot once start me.
>
> (5.5.10)

MACBETH REFLECTS CONTEMPORARY ISSUES

We realize that its medieval story of the rise and fall of a usurper has been colored by, and also in some sense mirrors, a number of contemporary interests and events. In 1605, for instance, just a year before the probable date of the play's composition and first performance, came the revelation of the Gunpowder Plot, a plan to blow up King, Lords, and Commons in Parliament as they convened for the new session of that year on the fifth of November. The plot was made known through an anonymous letter only ten days before the intended massacre, and the climate of shock and suspicion that prevailed throughout England, especially London, immediately thereafter has almost certainly left its mark in the play's haunted atmosphere of blood, darkness, stealth, treachery, and in the vividness with which it communicates the feeling that a whole community based on loyalty and trust has been thrown into terror by mysterious agencies (both unnatural and natural) working through it like a black yeast. Several of the conspirators were from Warwick, Shakespeare's own county, and may have been known to him. If so, there was no doubt personal as well as dramatic relevance in such observations of the play as Duncan's "There's no art To find the mind's construction in the face" (1.4.12), or Macbeth's "False face must hide what the false heart doth know" (1.7.82). At the very least, such statements, however they were meant by their author, would have held an exceptional charge of meaning for the play's first audiences in 1606.

Witchcraft, too, is among the contemporary interests that the play draws into its murderous web. Witchcraft was a live issue at all times in the sixteenth and seventeenth centuries, but it loomed especially large in the public mind after the Scottish James I came to power following the great Elizabeth, in 1603. James considered himself an authority on witches, had published a book on demonology in 1599 affirming their existence and their baleful influence in human affairs, and, in 1604, a year after his accession to the throne, inaugurated new statutes against them. Thus, the whole topic was accentuated at just about the time of the writing of the play.

Except in one phrase (1.3.6) and in the stage directions, the play always refers to the witches as *weyard*—or *weyward*—*sisters*. Both spellings are variations of *weird*, which in Shakespeare's time did not mean "freakish," but "fateful"—having to do with the determination of destinies. Shakespeare had met with such creatures in Holinshed, who regularly refers to the supernatural agents with whom Macbeth has dealings as "the three sisters," or "the three weird sisters," i.e., the three Fates. The witches in the play, however, are by no means so unambiguously defined. They have considerable power of insight and suggestion, we gather, but they do not determine a man's will, and Macbeth never blames them for influencing what he has done, only for tricking him into a false security. They are presented to us, moreover, in a climate of suggestion that is fully as demeaning as it is aggrandizing. If they belong with one part of their nature to an extra-human world of thunder, lightning, rain, and demonic powers (1.1), and, as Banquo says, "look not like th' inhabitants o' th' earth" (1.3.41), they have nevertheless some of the attributes of defeminized old women; their familiar demons assume shapes no more terrible than those of cat and toad; and the actions with which they identify themselves—killing swine, wheedling chestnuts, and persecuting the "rump-fed ronyon's"[1] (1.3.6) sea-going husband—show a pettishness and spite that seem perhaps more human than diabolical.

On the other hand, the weyard sisters are obviously more

1. ronyon: scabby creature

impressive than the ordinary garden variety of seventeenth-century witch, the village crone or hallucinated girl, and their collusion with such dire agents as Lady Macbeth calls upon (1.5.45) and Macbeth invokes (4.1.50) seems unmistakable. The obscurity with which Shakespeare envelops their nature and powers is very probably deliberate, since he seems to intend them to body forth, in a physical presence on stage, precisely the mystery, the ambiguity, the question mark (psychological as well as metaphysical) that lies at the root of human wrong-doing, which is always both local and explicable, universal and inexplicable, like these very figures. In their relations with Macbeth, they are obviously objective "real" beings with whom he talks. Yet they are also in some sense representative of potentialities within him and within the scheme of things of which he is a part.

What is emphatically to be noticed is that the weyard sisters do not suggest Duncan's murder; they simply make a prediction, and Macbeth himself takes the matter from there. The prediction they make, moreover, is entirely congenial to the situation, requires no special insight. Having made himself in this last battle more than ever the great warrior-hero of the kingdom and its chief defender, what more natural than that the ambitious man should be moved in the flush of victory to look ahead, hope, imagine? Hence, while recognizing the objectivity of the sisters as diabolical agents, we may also look on them as representing the potentialities for evil that lurk in every success, agents of a nemesis that seems to attend always on the more extreme dilations of the human ego.

Besides the lore of witchcraft, in which he was intensely interested, and the great Plot which threatened to destroy him together with his Parliament, James's own tenure of the English throne seems to be celebrated, at least obliquely, in Shakespeare's play. His family, the Stuarts, claimed descent from Banquo, and it is perhaps on this account that Shakespeare departs from Holinshed, in whose narrative Banquo is Macbeth's accomplice in the assassination of Duncan, to insist on his "royalty of nature" and the "dauntless temper of his mind" (3.1.50). Many critics see a notable compliment to James in the dumb show of kings descending from Banquo ["What, will the line stretch out to th' crack of doom?" (4.1.117)] which so appalls Macbeth at the cave of the weyard sisters. Some commentators, influenced by its Scottish background and its use of a story involving one of James's reputed ancestors, go so far as to suppose that the play was actually composed for a royal occasion and conceivably by royal command. What is certain, in any case, is that the playwright has effectively transformed a remote and primitive story—which at first looks simple—into a theatrical event tense with contemporary relevance. The almost routine assassination of a weak, good-natured king in Holinshed becomes, in Shakespeare's hands, a sensitive and terrifying exposition of the abyss a man may open in himself and in the entire sum of things by a naked act of self-will.

MACBETH REFLECTS WELL-KNOWN MYTH AND FOLKLORE

This brings us to the third face of *Macbeth*, its character as parable, as myth. For all its medieval plot and its framework of Jacobean feeling, the play has a universal theme: the consuming nature of pride, the rebellion it incites to, the destruction it brings. In some ways Shakespeare's story resembles the story of the Fall of Satan. Macbeth has imperial longings, as Satan has; he is started on the road to revolt partly by the circumstance that another is placed above him; he attempts to bend the universe to his will, warring against all the bonds that relate men to each other—reverence, loyalty, obedience, truth, justice, mercy, and love. But again, as in Satan's case, to no avail. The principles his actions violate prove in the event stronger than he, knit up the wounds he has made in them, and combine to plunge him into an isolation, or alienation, that reveals itself (not only in social and political but in psychological terms) to be a kind of Hell. As [poet John] Milton's Satan was to put it later in *Paradise Lost:* "Which way I fly is Hell; myself am Hell."

In other ways, the story Shakespeare tells may remind us of the folktale of which [playwright Christopher] Marlowe's *Dr. Faustus* is one version: a man sells his soul to the Devil in return for superhuman powers only to find in the end that his gains are illusory, his losses unbearable. It is true, of course, that Shakespeare's hero is attracted by the Scottish throne, not by magic or by power in general; and it is likewise true that he signs no formal contract like his predecessor. Still, the resemblances remain. Macbeth does open his mind to diabolical promptings:

This supernatural soliciting
Cannot be ill, cannot be good. If ill,

Why hath it given me earnest of success,
Commencing in a truth? I am Thane of Cawdor.
If good, why do I yield to that suggestion
Whose horrid image doth unfix my hair
And make my seated heart knock at my ribs
Against the use of nature?

(1.3.130)

He imagines himself, moreover, to have received immunities of a superhuman sort:

I will not be afraid of death and bane
Till Birnam Forest come to Dunsinane.

(5.3.59)

But swords I smile at, weapons laugh to scorn,
Brandished by man that's of a woman born.

(5.7.12)

And he finds in the end, like Faustus, that his gains amount to nothing:

I have lived long enough. My way of life
Is fall'n into the sere, the yellow leaf,
And that which should accompany old age,
As honor, love, obedience, troops of friends,
I must not look to have; but, in their stead,
Curses not loud but deep, mouth-honor, breath,
Which the poor heart would fain deny, and dare not.

(5.3.22)

The very immunities he thought had been guaranteed him prove deceptive, for Birnam Wood comes to high Dunsinane after all, and so does an antagonist not born of woman in the usual sense. In the end, Macbeth knows that what he had begun to fear after Duncan's murder, in the course of meditating Banquo's, is true: he has given his soul to the Devil to make the descendants of Banquo, not his own descendants, kings. All his plans have become instrumental to a larger plan that is not his:

They hailed him father to a line of kings.
Upon my head they placed a fruitless crown
And put a barren sceptre in my gripe,
Thence to be wrenched with an unlineal hand,
No son of mine succeeding. If 't be so,
For Banquo's issue have I filed my mind;
For them the gracious Duncan have I murdered,
Put rancors in the vessel of my peace
Only for them, and mine eternal jewel
Given to the common enemy of man
To make them kings—the seeds of Banquo kings.

(3.1.60)

THE MACBETHS RESEMBLE MILTON'S ADAM AND EVE

As [psychoanalyst Sigmund] Freud noticed long ago, the two Macbeths complement each other in their reactions to the crime. Her fall is instantaneous, even eager, like Eve's in *Paradise Lost;* his is gradual and reluctant, like Adam's. She needs only her husband's letter about the weyard sisters' prophecy to precipitate her resolve to kill Duncan. Within an instant she is inviting murderous spirits to unsex her, fill her with cruelty, thicken her blood, convert her mother's milk to gall, and darken the world "That my keen knife see not the wound it makes" (1.5.50). Macbeth, in contrast, vacillates. The images of the deed that possess him simultaneously repel him (1.3.130, 1.7.1). When she proposes Duncan's murder, he temporizes: "We will speak further" (1.5.69).

Later, withdrawing from the supper they have laid for Duncan to consider the matter alone, he very nearly decides not to proceed. It takes all her intensity, all her scorn of what she wrongly chooses to call unmanliness, to steel him to the deed. Throughout this first crime, we notice, it is she who assumes the initiative and devises what is to be done (1.5.64, 1.7.60). Yet we would certainly be wrong to see her as monster or fiend. On the contrary, she is perhaps more than usually feminine. She is conscious of her woman's breasts, her mother's milk (1.5.45); knows "How tender 'tis to love the babe that milks me" (1.7.55); and, when she thinks to carry out the murder herself, fails because the sleeping King too much reminds her of her father (2.2.12). We may infer from this that she is no strapping Amazon; Macbeth calls her his dearest "chuck" (3.2.45), and she speaks, when sleep-walking, of her "little hand" (5.1.48). Thus such evidence as there is suggests that we are to think of her as a womanly woman, capable of great natural tenderness, but one who, for the sake of her husband's advancement and probably her own, has now wound up her will almost to the breaking point.

An equally important contrast between the two Macbeths appears sharply in the scene following the murder, one of the most powerful scenes that Shakespeare ever wrote. Their difference of response at this point is striking—not only because he is shaken to the core and cannot conceal it, whereas she shows an iron discipline throughout, but also because his imagination continues as in the past to be attuned to a world of experience that is closed to her. That world is visionary and even hallucinatory, we can readily see, but at the same time, it is the mark of a keener moral sense, a fuller consciousness of the implications of what they have done, than she possesses. The difference between his and her responses is related to a form of double vision that extends throughout the play. Shakespeare establishes for us from the beginning one perspective on his story that is symbolic and mythical, a perspective that includes both the objective weyard sisters, on the one hand, and the subjective images of horror and retribution that rise like smoke from Macbeth's protesting imagination, on the other. The play also establishes, as a second perspective, the ordinary historical world of Scotland, where Duncan is king, Macbeth becomes king, Malcolm will be king, and the witches are skinny old women with beards. In general, Macbeth enacts his crimes in the historical world, experiences them in the symbolic world, and out of this experience, new crimes arise to be enacted in the former. To put it in different terms, a force that seems to come from outside the time-world of history impinges on history, converting history into an experience for Macbeth that is timeless and mythical. We are asked to sense that his crime is not simply a misdeed in the secular political society of a given time and place, but simultaneously a rupture in some dimly apprehended ultimate scheme of things where our material world of evil *versus* good and virtue *versus* vice gives way to a spiritual world of sin *versus* grace and hell *versus* heaven.

PHYSICAL AND METAPHYSICAL IMPLICATIONS

The suggestiveness of Shakespeare's play in this larger sense is inexhaustible. Every element it contains lives with a double life, one physical, one metaphysical. Consider night for instance. Night settles down halfway through the first act and stays there through much of the rest of the play: 1.6–7, 2.1–4, 3.2–5, 4.1, and 5.1 are night scenes, and several more, undetermined in the text, could be effectively presented as such, e.g., 1.5 and 4.2–3. All this is ordinary nighttime, of course, but it is obviously much more. "Thick," "murky," full of "fog and filthy air," it "entombs" the face of earth (2.4.9), blots out the stars and the moon, "strangles" even the sun (2.4.7). Duncan rides into it to his death, as does Banquo. Lady Macbeth evokes it (1.5.48) and then finds herself its prisoner, endlessly sleepwalking through the thick night of a darkened mind.

Macbeth succumbs to its embrace so completely that, in the end, even a "night-shriek" cannot stir him.

Or again, consider blood. "What bloody man is that?" are the play's first words, following the first weyard sisters' scene. Like the night, blood is both ordinary and special. It sticks like real blood: "His secret murders sticking on his hands," says Angus of Macbeth (5.2.17). It smells as real blood smells: "Here's the smell of the blood still," says Lady Macbeth (5.1.47) hopelessly washing. Yet it finally covers everything Macbeth has touched, in ways both qualitative and quantitative that real blood could not. The sleeping grooms are "all badged" with it, their daggers "Unmannerly breeched with gore." Duncan's silver skin is "laced" with it (2.3.108), Banquo's murderer has it on his face (3.4.14), Banquo's hair is "boltered" with it (4.1.123), and Macbeth's feet are soaked in it (3.4.136). Perhaps the two most bloodcurdling lines in the play, when expressively spoken, are Macbeth's lines after the ghost of Banquo is gone: "It will have blood, they say: blood will have blood" (3.4.122) and Lady Macbeth's moaning cry as she washes and washes: "Yet who would have thought the old man to have had so much blood in him?" (5.1.35).

Macbeth's style of speech in the play has something of this same double character. The startling thing about much of it is its inwardness, as if it were spoken not with the voice at all, but somewhere deep in the arteries and veins, communing with remote strange powers.

> Light thickens, and the crow
> Makes wing to th' rooky wood;
> Good things of day begin to droop and drowse,
> Whiles night's black agents to their preys do rouse.
>
> (3.2.50)

Between the two battles that open and close the play, Macbeth's language seems frequently to lean away from the historical world of Scotland toward the registering of such experience as rises, timeless and spaceless, both from within his mind and beyond it. Thence come thronging those images that "unfix my hair" (1.3.135), the presences that will "blow the horrid deed in every eye" (1.7.24), the voices that cry "Sleep no more!" (2.2.34), the ghost that returns from the dead to mock him for what he has failed to achieve, and the apparitions that are called with great effort from some nether (but also inner) world only to offer him the very counsels that he most wants to hear.

These continuous blurrings of the "real" with the "unreal," intrusions of what is past and supposedly finished into the present (Banquo's ghost, 3.4), and even into the theoretically still formless future (Banquo's descendants, 4.1), provide an appropriate sort of environment for Macbeth and his wife. Lady Macbeth is easily "transported," we learn from her first words to her husband, "beyond This ignorant present" to feel "The future in the instant" (1.5.54). In a similar way, Macbeth's imagination leaps constantly from what is now to what is to come, from the weyard sisters' prophecy to Duncan's murder, from being "thus" to being "safely thus" (3.1.48), from the menace of Banquo to the menace of Macduff, and from a today that is known to an unknown "To-morrow, and to-morrow, and to-morrow" (5.5.19). Shakespeare vividly records in these ways the restlessness of the Macbeths' ambition and at the same time the problem that ambition, like every other natural urge to self-realization, poses for human beings and their relationships to each other.

THE SIGNIFICANCE OF FEASTS AND CHILDREN

To understand this problem in the dramatic and poetic terms Shakespeare gives it, it is helpful to look at two of the play's most often noticed features. One is feasting. Macbeth withdraws from the supper he has laid for Duncan to weigh the arguments for killing him (1.7). The entertainment, which he has himself ordered, marks his adherence to the community of mutual service that we find implied in the scene at Duncan's court (1.4). Here is a society, we realize, that depends on thane cherishing king—"The service and the loyalty I owe," Macbeth tells Duncan, "In doing it pays itself"—and on king cherishing thane: "I have begun to plant thee," Duncan assures Macbeth, "and will labor To make thee full of growing" (1.4.28). When Macbeth withdraws, therefore, we see him retreating from the shared community of the supper that he has provided for Duncan and the other thanes into the isolation that his intended crime against that community implies. Once he has withdrawn and his withdrawal is sealed by murder, he can never rejoin the community he has ruptured. This he discovers at the feast in 3.4, when the ghost of Banquo preempts his place. The only community left him after this is the community of dark powers we see him appealing to in 4.1, where the weyard sisters dance about a hell-broth (also a feast?) of dislocated fragments. After 3.4, we never see Macbeth in the company of more than one or two other persons, usually servants, and in the last act his forces ebb inexorably away till there is only himself. Similarly, and with similar implications, after 3.4 we never see Macbeth and his wife together. Instead of being united by the crime, they are increasingly separated by it, she gradually lost in the inner hell that she finds so "murky" in the sleepwalking scene, he always busier in the outer hell that he has made Scotland into.

The other much commented on feature is children. Four children have roles in the play: Donalbain, Malcolm, Fleance, and the son of Macduff. Two children are among the apparitions raised by the weyard sisters in 4.1: "a Bloody Child" and "a Child Crowned, with a tree in his hand." Allusions to children occur often. We hear of the child or children Lady Macbeth must have sometime had (1.7.54), of the son Macbeth wishes he had now to succeed him (3.1.64), and of pity, who comes "like a naked new-born babe Striding the blast" to trumpet forth Macbeth's murderous act till "tears shall drown the wind" (1.7.21). Plainly, in some measure, all these "children" relate to what the play is telling us about time. Macbeth, in his Scottish world (though not in his demonic one), belongs like the rest of us to a world of time: he has been Glamis, he is Cawdor, and he shall be (so the weyard sisters predict) "King hereafter" (1.3.50). The crux, of course, is *hereafter*. Macbeth and his wife seek to make hereafter now, to wrench the future into the present by main force, to master time. But this option, the play seems to be saying, is always disastrous for human beings. The only way human beings can constructively master time is Banquo's way, letting it grow and unfold from the present as the Stuart line of kings is to grow and unfold from Fleance. The more Macbeth seeks to control the future, the more it counters and defeats him (in Fleance, Donalbain, Malcolm, the bloody child, the crowned child) and the more he is himself cut off from its creative unfolding processes—having *had* children we are told, but having now only a "fruitless" crown, a "barren" scepter. "No son of mine succeeding" (3.1.64).

Toward the play's end, Malcolm and his soldiers move in on Dunsinane with their "leavy screens" (5.6.1), and very soon after this Macduff, the man who "was from his mother's womb Untimely ripped," meets Macbeth (5.8), slays him, then reappears with his head fixed on a pike. What did Shakespeare in-

tend us to make of this? All that can be said for certain is that
the situation on stage in these scenes has some sort of allusive
relation to the three apparitions that were summoned at Macbeth's wish by the weyard sisters. The first was an armed
head—matched here at the play's end, apparently, by Macbeth's armed head on a pike. The second was a bloody child,
who told him that none of woman born could harm him. This
child is evidently to be associated with Macduff. The third apparition was a crowned child holding a tree—an allusion, we
may suppose, to Malcolm, child of Duncan, who is soon to be
crowned King, who is part of the future that Macbeth has tried
in vain to control, and who now with his men, holding the
green branches of Birnam Wood, seems calculated to remind
us of the way in which Nature, green, fertile, "full of growing,"
(1.4.29) moves inexorably to "overgrow" a man who has more
and more identified himself with death and all such destructive uses of power as the armed head suggests.

If these speculations are at all well-founded, what takes
place in the final scenes is that a kind of Living Death, a figure who has alienated himself from all the growing
processes, goes out to war encased in an armor that he believes to be invulnerable on the ground that nothing in the
scheme of nature, nothing born of woman, can conquer
Death. But he is wrong. Death can always be conquered by
the bloody child, who, being ripped from the womb as his
mother lay dying, is indicative of the life that in Nature's
scheme of things (like the green leaves in Birnam Wood) is
always being reborn from death.

STAGING DEVICES DRAMATIZE MACBETH'S DOWNFALL

To leave the play on this abstract and allegorical plane, however,
is to do it wrong. What comes home most sharply to us as we
watch these last scenes performed is the twistings and turnings
of a ruined but fascinating human being, a human being capable of profound even if disbalanced insights, probing the bound-
aries of our common nature ever more deeply in frantically
changing accesses of arrogance and despair, defiance and cow-
ardice, lethargy and exhilaration, folly and wisdom. Underscor-
ing this, we have the succession of abrupt changes from place to
place, group to group, and speaker to speaker that marks scenes
2 to 8 in Act 5, an unsettling discontinuity which does much to
dramatize our sense of a kingdom coming apart at the seams. In
the background, too, we hear the gradually swelling underbeat

of the allied drums, called for by the stage directions in 5.2, 4, 6, and 8, and audible elsewhere if the director desires. This gives a sensory dimension to the increasing prosperity of Malcolm's cause, and can be made particularly dramatic and significant in 5.5. Here, following the scene's opening, we hear Macbeth's drums for the only time in the play. Then comes the famous soliloquy, where he assures us that life is an empty fraud, a "tale told by an idiot." If, at the close of this, when the door to Dunsinane opens to admit the messenger bearing the news of Birnam Wood, we hear again in the distance the steady beat of the allied drums signifying the existence of a very different point of view about the value of life, the impact is powerful.

Perhaps the most telling sensory effect in these final scenes is the call of trumpets. We hear them first on the appearance of Macduff, whose command may remind us of Macbeth's earlier prognostication about "heaven's cherubin" riding the winds and blowing the fame—or infamy—of the murder of Duncan through the whole world:

> Make all our trumpets speak, give them all breath,
> Those clamorous harbingers of blood and death.
>
> (5.6.9)

We then hear their alarums with the next entry of Macduff, who is now searching for Macbeth, and again with the exist of Malcolm; alarums once more when Macduff and Macbeth begin to fight and when they go fighting off stage; and finally, three massed flourishes of trumpets, one as Malcolm enters after the sounding of retreat, a second as Macduff and the other thanes hail Malcolm king, and a third as all go out, Macbeth's head waving somberly on Macduff's spear (5.8.35). The former age has been wiped away and the new age inaugurated, fittingly, to the sound of the trumpets of a Judgment.

All this, we understand, is as it must be. Alike as ruler and man, Macbeth has been tried and found wanting. Yet we realize, as we hear Malcolm speak of "this dead butcher and his fiend-like queen" (5.8.69)—and we realize it all the more because of these last scenes, in which a great man goes down fighting, bayed around by enemies external and internal, natural and even supernatural, committed to the Father of Lies but taking the consequences like a man—how much there is that judgment does not know, and how much there is that, through Shakespeare's genius, we do.

A Renaissance Perspective of the Witches

Francis Fergusson

Francis Fergusson portrays *Macbeth*'s Witches as representatives of unnatural power whose presence heightens the tension of the play when Macbeth meets them. Fergusson explains Renaissance knowledge and beliefs about witches, who were seen as crazed old women possessed by minor evil spirits called Familiars. Because their power is limited, they use ambiguous talk and apparitions to tease Macbeth into destroying himself. Francis Fergusson, a theater director, editor, and author of poetry, plays, and criticism, taught at Bennington College and Princeton, Rutgers, and Indiana Universities. He is the author of *Trope and Allegory: Themes Common to Dante and Shakespeare* and *The Idea of a Theatre: A Study of Ten Plays.*

[*Macbeth*] is the shortest and most concentrated of the tragedies, and Shakespeare gets it under way with more than his usual speed. The brief appearance of the Witches (Act I, scene 1) suggests that unnatural powers are abroad, seeking Macbeth; their childish doggerel, "Fair is foul, and foul is fair," tells us that things are not what they seem in Scotland. . . .

THE EFFECT OF THE WITCHES ON MACBETH

It is when we meet Macbeth (scene 3) that the action of the play begins to take on its full power. He and Banquo, leaving the field of battle, meet the Witches, who have been expecting them; and Macbeth's first line echoes the Witches' chant of scene 1: "So fair and foul a day I have not seen." Macbeth is not only the protagonist, he is also the character who sees

Reprinted from Francis Fergusson, *Shakespeare: The Pattern in His Carpet,* Delacorte Press, 1970. Copyright © 1958, 1959, 1960, 1961, 1963, 1965, 1966, 1967, 1968, and 1970 by Francis Fergusson. Used by permission of Delacorte Press, a division of Bantam Doubleday Dell Publishing Group, Inc.

most deeply into what is going on. It has often been pointed out that he is both a powerful and ambitious warrior, and a suffering poet and seer. . . .

When the Witches tell him (Act I, scene 3) that he will be Thane of Cawdor, and then King, they feed the secret dream he had shared only with his Lady. When Ross greets him as Thane of Cawdor, he is caught up—"rapt," as Banquo notices—in a vision of supreme power:

> Two truths are told,
> As happy prologues to the swelling act
> Of the imperial theme.

But he knows, in a moment, that the Witches' truth is double-edged:

> This supernatural soliciting
> Cannot be ill, cannot be good.

And he sees, with dismay, that it has overpowered him:

> . . . why do I yield to that suggestion,
> Whose horrid image doth unfix my hair,
> And make my seated heart knock at my ribs,
> Against the use of nature?

RENAISSANCE KNOWLEDGE OF WITCHES

The experience of Macbeth and his Lady is, of course, the center of the play. But it is revealed to us in its wider meanings through two complementary themes, that of the Witches, who start the whole action, and that of Ross, Malcolm, and Macduff, who find their way out of the Scottish hell and end Macbeth's career.

The Witches as actually written by Shakespeare are only the three Weird Sisters; Hecate is a late addition by [dramatist Thomas] Middleton. With Hecate out of the way, the dramatic and poetic style of the Witch scenes is consistent. And in the light of recent studies we can understand how Shakespeare saw them as stage figures.

He found the Witches and their equivocal prophecies in [historian Raphael] Holinshed but developed them according to the popular lore of the time. The Renaissance knew a bewildering variety of witches and magicians, creatures of Latin legend, Norse mythology, and the folklore of northern Europe. We cannot tell whether Shakespeare "believed" in any of this; but we can see that he used it in the play to make the Witches actable, and recognizable to his audience, and at the same time to suggest, behind them, further unseen powers of evil.

When the Witches first appear (Act I, scene 1) we gather that they have been summoned by their Familiars: "I come, Graymalkin"; "Paddock calls." Familiars were minor evil spirits who took possession of old women or other susceptible types, thus making them "witches." Witches had to obey their Familiars, but received in return some power to do mischief themselves, to travel by air, and to sail in sieves. Shakespeare apparently did not show the Familiars onstage, since they are not mentioned in the cast or in stage directions; their presence is indicated only by what the Witches say and by offstage cries and whines. According to folklore, Graymalkin is a cat, Paddock a toad, urchin, or "hedgepig," and Harpier an owl. Through their Familiars the Witches are associated with supernatural powers, the Norns (the Fates of Norse mythology), or Satan himself. But they are not themselves supernatural. They are old women, seduced and thwarted by the spirits they adore and serve.

As old women crazily inspired by evil, the Witches are extremely actable, and far more uncanny than they would be under gauze, with a spooky green light on them. Their appetite for mischief is infinite, but what they can accomplish in that line is limited. The first Witch yearns in vain (Act I, scene 3) to sink the homecoming Pilot's ship, but she can only torment him:

Weary sev'nights, nine times nine,
Shall he dwindle, peak, and pine.
Though his bark cannot be lost,
Yet it shall be tempest-tossed.

In these lines we hear the teasing whine of one who is herself teased. We hear it more piercingly in the half-truths with which the Witches tempt Macbeth. Unable to ruin him directly, they must tease him into ruining himself. They crave to subject him to the frustrations they suffer, much as Iago craves to subject Othello to the envy and hatred which possess him. There is humor in Shakespeare's conception of the Witches: with their mocking nursery-rhymes, they are queer childish images of Macbeth's terrible futility.

The Witches' charms and incantations are traditional magic. In their final scene (Act IV, scene 1) all that they do is significant at showing their bond with evil. They appear, as before, in response to the mew, the whine, and the cry of their Familiars; but thereafter they deal with their "masters"— probably more potent spirits. The apparitions they show

Macbeth, in the form of bodies or parts of bodies, are "necromancy,"[1] supposedly the best kind of prophecy. They show in this scene the utmost their "art" can accomplish, stirring the cauldron, making their circles, and adding the ingredients according to the recipes of classical demonology. They are treating Macbeth with new respect because they know that Macbeth himself now has status in hell. Like Faust,[2] Macbeth has "mine eternal jewel/ Given to the common enemy of man." Moreover he has seen that he has probably sold his soul in vain, for Banquo rose from the dead to plague him (Act III, scene 4) and Banquo's son escaped for all his efforts. That point—the banquet scene and its aftermath—marks the climax and turning point in Macbeth's action. He has no hope of winning, nor can he turn back:

> I am in blood
> Stepped in so far, that should I wade no more,
> Returning were as tedious as go o'er—

the dreariest version of his nightmare race. Now (after the banquet scene), he is "bent to know/ By the worst means the worst," and he commands the Witches to show it to him even though "destruction sicken."

The Witches are his to command; yet they contrive to play with him a little longer. The apparitions are arranged in such a way as to make him hope, then despair, then hope again. Then they finish him off in triumph: "Show!/ Show!/ Show!/ Show his eyes, and grieve his heart./ Come like shadows, so depart."

The apparitions refer in their ambiguous way to Macbeth's fate as it actually overtakes him in Act V. They also suggest the nature of Macbeth's crimes, the judgment of God upon them, and the return of the pretty world once he is gone. They are announced by thunder, a sign of the voice of God since the most ancient times. Macbeth half understands that himself; he wants to "tell pale-hearted fear it lies;/ And sleep in spite of thunder." The Armed Head means Macbeth himself (whose head is cut off in the end) and Macduff, who kills him. The Bloody Child also means Macduff, of course; and it is a reminder of Lady Macbeth's babe (Act I, scene 7) whose boneless gums she is prepared to pluck from her nipple to dash its brains out; and Macbeth's "pity, like a naked,

1. the practice of supposedly communicating with the spirits of the dead in order to predict the future 2. the central character in plays by Marlowe and Goethe; a magician and alchemist in German legend who sells his soul to the devil in exchange for power and knowledge

newborn babe" whom he was about to violate by murder. Shakespeare often uses children as the most touching and natural symbol of new life and hope; in this scene they suggest both what Macbeth was trying to kill, and his ultimate failure. The "Child, crowned, with a tree in his hand," carries all these meanings. He means Banquo's issue; the tree is the genealogical tree of the Scottish kings all the way down to James. The tree also means Birnam Wood, and as such gives Macbeth false hope. And the leafy tree is a symbol as old, and as universal, as thunder, for the springtime renewal of life itself. It occurs in countless primitive festivals which

---

THE WITCHES' FOUR APPARITIONS

In act 4, scene 1, Macbeth seeks the Witches' prophecy. He sees four apparitions, three of which the Witches explain in riddles Macbeth misinterprets.

   Thunder. FIRST APPARITION, *an Armed Head.*
 MACB. Tell me, thou unknown power—
 1. WITCH.   He knows thy thought.
Hear his speech, but say thou naught.
 1. APPAR. Macbeth! Macbeth! Macbeth! Beware
  Macduff;
Beware the Thane of Fife. Dismiss me. Enough.
          He descends.
 MACB. Whate'er thou art, for thy good caution thanks!
Thou hast harp'd my fear aright. But one word more—
 1. WITCH. He will not be commanded. Here's another,
More potent than the first.
 Thunder. SECOND APPARITION, *a Bloody Child.*
 2. APPAR. Macbeth! Macbeth! Macbeth!
 MACB. Had I three ears, I'ld hear thee.
 2. APPAR. Be bloody, bold, and resolute; laugh to
  scorn
The pow'r of man, for none of woman born
Shall harm Macbeth.
          Descends.
 MACB. Then live, Macduff. What need I fear of thee?
But yet I'll make assurance double sure
And take a bond of fate. Thou shalt not live!
That I may tell pale-hearted fear it lies
And sleep in spite of thunder.
   [*Thunder.* THIRD APPARITION, *A Child Crowned, with
     a tree in his hand.*]

mark the death of Old Man Winter and the joyful birth of his successor. Shakespeare was familiar with it, as the Maypole, in the spring festivals all over England. It is still used in country districts.

These visions reveal what is going on in Macbeth's suffering, perceptive mind and spirit, and they are connected with the imagery of his monologues. In this respect they are like the premonitions of disaster that Shakespeare so often grants to his tragic protagonists in the fourth act of the tragedy. But by means of the Witches he gives them a kind of objective reality: behind them we can make out the whole

> What is this
> That rises like the issue of a king
> And wears upon his baby-brow the round
> And top of sovereignty?
> ALL.   Listen, but speak not to't.
> 3. APPAR. Be lion-mettled, proud, and take no care
> Who chafes, who frets, or where conspirers are.
> Macbeth shall never vanquish'd be until
> Great Birnam Wood to high Dunsinane Hill
> Shall come against him.   *Descends.*
> MACB.   That will never be.
> Who can impress the forest, bid the tree
> Unfix his earth-bound root? Sweet bodements, good!
> Rebellion's head rise never till the Wood
> Of Birnam rise, and our high-plac'd Macbeth
> Shall live the lease of nature, pay his breath
> To time and mortal custom. Yet my heart
> Throbs to know one thing. Tell me, if your art
> Can tell so much—Shall Banquo's issue ever
> Reign in this kingdom?
> ALL.   Seek to know no more
> MACB. I will be satisfied. Deny me this,
> And an eternal curse fall on you! Let me know.
> Why sinks that cauldron? and what noise is this?
>   *Hautboys.*
> 1. WITCH. Show!
> 2. WITCH. Show!
> 3. WITCH. Show!
> ALL. Show his eyes, and grieve his heart!
> Come like shadows, so depart!
>   *A show of eight Kings, the eighth with a glass in his*
>   *hand, and* BANQUO *last.*

ordered world of Shakespeare's tradition, violated by Macbeth, and now returning in triumph.

The Witches disappear as the endless procession of Kings begins, to the sound of hautboys,[3] and we never see them again. Macbeth returns with a bump to present reality, and instantly hears "the galloping of horse," the windy sound of the losing race which is all he has to look forward to. We do not see him again until the final sequences in Dunsinane (Act V). The rest of Act IV and much of Act V are dominated by Malcolm, Macduff, and Ross, who reverse the hellish course of events and end Macbeth's career.

3. Oboes

CHAPTER 2

Producing *Macbeth* Onstage

READINGS ON
MACBETH

Three Stage Productions of *Macbeth*

David A. Male

David A. Male argues that the director of a stage production has a governing idea in mind, suggested to the
audience by means of the details of setting, costumes,
and acting. Male analyzes three productions of *Macbeth*
and shows how each director's set and presentation of
the Witches resulted in two different religious interpretations and one political interpretation of the play. David
A. Male directs plays in a theater of his own design and
has taught drama in state-supported schools in England
and at Homeston College in Cambridge, England. He is
the author of *The Story of the Theatre*, *Approaches to
Drama*, and *Investigating Drama*.

Speaking to the company during a rehearsal for his production
of *Macbeth* in 1967, Peter Hall aired this view of the play:

> A lot of people say it's the most Christian play Shakespeare ever
> wrote, first because of the basic and real holiness of Duncan
> and of Edward the Confessor; but also the text is littered with
> echoes of the authorised version of the bible, biblical images,
> and because Macbeth himself is conscious of damnation in a
> way in which no other Shakespeare hero is.
>
> (Programme Note R.S.C. *Macbeth* 1967)

This forcefully expressed and specific assessment of the
play is but one example of the range of responses by directors
to the text. To understand fully a particular production it becomes vital to recognise what the director sees as central in
importance in the play, in other words, what is his governing
idea. This decision, which needs to be perceived by the audience, has significant implications in many aspects of the production, notably the general setting . . . [and] the nature of the
Witches and all their paraphernalia of black magic. . . .

From David A. Male, *Macbeth: Shakespeare on Stage* (New York: Cambridge University
Press, 1984). Copyright © 1984 by Cambridge University Press. Reprinted by permission of Cambridge University Press.

The 1974 production, directed by Trevor Nunn, presented the play as a battle between Good and Evil. Duncan represented a harmonious, ordered, Christian society, of which he was the saint-like head. Macbeth with the Witches represented the evil of Satan and Black Magic which created discord and disorder. This religious atmosphere was greatly intensified by setting the play within a church.

A production two years later, not in the main theatre at Stratford, but in the smaller theatre, The Other Place, again by Trevor Nunn, still presented the play as a battlefield of the sacred against the profane, but the emphasis was more sharply focussed on Macbeth and his wife. One critic wrote: 'The first half of the play had the scheming couple looking outward into a world they see as their oyster and then . . . that outside world (is) no oyster but a giant octopus closing in on them.'

There was a conspicuous absence of any religious references in Howard Davies' production in 1982. Here the atmosphere was very much down to earth. Scotland was full of noblemen who were essentially selfish, ambitious, ready to make alliances only for political convenience. Evil in the play was not associated with Satan but attributed to man's personal, aggressive ambition. With the removal of the spiritual or magical elements found in the earlier productions, the play presented a political society governed by worldly, tough soldiers.

These contrasting approaches to the play gave each production a very different emphasis, achieved in very distinctive ways. It is worth noting that though Macbeth actually reigned as a Scottish king and Holinshed's account provides a historical record of the main events, not one of the directors saw the play as a drama about the throne of Scotland. Indeed little attempt was made even to suggest a Scottish environment in the settings or vocal accents. The focus was very clearly on the much more personal tragedy of Macbeth's ambitious designs and their ultimate failure. As a consequence, the settings were used as a means to demonstrate the tragedy rather than recreate a history. The settings of the play revealed the distinctive focus that each director had selected for his central emphasis. In our detailed examination of these three productions we will look at the settings chosen in order to explore these different approaches. . . .

THE SETTINGS

In 1974, the play was set inside a partially ruined church chancel, furnished with side pews and a high altar flanked with massive candlesticks. Above was a huge chandelier. The church-like atmosphere was highlighted by a splendid religious ritual at the opening of the play—the coronation of King Duncan. Three huge banners arranged as an altar triptych[1] provided a background for the kneeling King. Bathed in brilliant white light, the gold robed, white surpliced, blind monarch received his crown. Black cassocked attendants (including Macbeth) stood in the darkened background which intensified the King's golden-white glory and saintly purity. Suddenly the atmosphere changed. A hurriedly drawn traverse curtain became a screen on which were thrown shadows of destruction. Duncan was attacked by an unidentified enemy wielding the altar crucifix as his weapon. The Witches were discovered riding on the great chandelier and with their descent the whole setting was transformed into a devilish meeting-place to celebrate a black mass. Chanting their exchanges as if participating in a demonic ritual, they produced their own black magic instruments squatting on a circle of dirty cloth.

The setting at the very opening created a specifically religious environment for the play. Duncan was given a saint-like character, Christ's redemption of Man through His sacrifice on the Cross was symbolised by the huge crucifix placed on the altar. The interruption by the Witches represented the reverse of that Christian image. The crucifix became a weapon to strike Duncan. The holy place was turned into a resort for witchcraft. With that opening sequence, the director established a double image. One face portrayed Christian order, and the reverse, devilish disorder. Later in the play we find objects being put to this double use. The altar at which Duncan's coronation took place became the banqueting table at which Macbeth's ascent to the throne was celebrated. The wine used for the banquet was contained in one huge bowl resembling the chalice used to hold the wine for Holy Communion. Both the table and the bowl were used as objects having a spiritual meaning and then were associated with Macbeth's very unChristian murder of Duncan and his assumption of kingship.

A very powerful contrast was achieved in giving Duncan such a saint-like, pious character. Macbeth became very much like the fallen angel Lucifer, at first the dutiful servant

1. a work of three hinged panels

and then the usurper. After the murder, Macbeth exchanged his black cassock for an aggressively scarlet robe which suggested the Devil incarnate. Indeed, a symbolic colour scheme was employed throughout the production. This moved from the white and gold of saintly innocence through the red and black of Macbeth's temporary tyranny to the reemergence of purity in the white cloaks worn for Malcolm's concluding Victory speech. All the costumes were military in style with long black greatcoats decorated with brass buttons, and trousers thrust into jackboots. Apart from subdued tartan sashes worn by the King's sons, there was no other Scottish reference.

The setting in 1976 could not have provided a more striking contrast, though the director was again Trevor Nunn. The play was performed in the box-like auditorium at Stratford called The Other Place, which had very limited technical facilities. The flat floor was surrounded on three sides by raked benches and a balcony to accommodate the audience. A painted black circle marked out the acting area. An outer ring created by plain, undisguised beer crates served as seats for actors waiting to perform, though the boxes were occasionally brought on stage either as stools for the banquet or to create the battlements of Dunsinane. Three other properties remained permanently on view: a giant thunder sheet, a huge bell and, on a wooden frame just outside the circle, the glittering golden coronation cope.[2] The wall of the theatre facing the audience was covered in plain wooden boarding with a very narrow central entrance.

The black painted circle was the most prominent feature of the setting and it suggested an evil world dominated by the three Witches. Inside that charmed circle, the characters appeared to be vulnerable to their evil intentions. The director intensified the visual focus of the circle by making the actors sit round its circumference looking at the scenes in which they did not take part. This watching pattern was carefully choreographed, as one critic wrote: 'the spectators were carefully chosen, the witches observe Macbeth as he demeans himself, Macduff is just outside the arena when his family are murdered within it . . . what is impressive is not the invention but the selection and refinements.' So the bodies of the watching actors became important elements in the setting.

As in 1974, the costumes were very military. The main characters wore black leather coats, high-necked tunics,

2. cloak or vestment

breeches and riding boots while some of the nobles were dressed in civilian court dress. The dominating colour of the whole production as well as the costumes was deadly black, relieved by a little grey or white and the occasional flash of tartan. Even for the banquet Lady Macbeth kept her grey/black costume, the only additional ornament being a small gold circlet worn over a tightly wrapped headscarf.

The visual approach of the 1982 production was completely different from the previous presentations. The venue was the main Stratford theatre. The walls surrounding the stage were stark black. The stage itself jutted into the audience, a small number of whom sat very close to the left and right hand edges. The acting space was dominated by a vast metal scaffold supporting a wide upper gallery reached by iron staircases, one coming forward towards the audience, the other giving rear access to the upper level. Wired-glass, semitransparent panels could be slid into positions in the frame of the scaffold that closed, or partially closed, off the rear section of the stage. When they were withdrawn the total expanse of the whole stage to the back wall was opened up. A pair of musicians sat in front of sets of percussion instruments: drums, bells, cymbals, xylophones. They became part of the visual effect, since they were permanently in position at each side of the gallery. Atmospheric percussive music accompanied much of the action and counterpointed many speeches. The silver glitter of the various instruments lightened the sombre, flat blackness of the metal structure and the dull reflections of the glassy panels. Movement on the metal was always noisy and echoing. There was nothing regal, religious or Scottish about the location.

Whilst the banquet scene in the earlier productions placed the nobles round a single table or squatting on boxes, in 1982 the thanes sat in pairs at separate tables grouped in a roughly circular shape. This skilful arrangement enabled Lady Macbeth to sit separately from the nobles, allowed Macbeth's wish to 'sit i' the midst,' as well as providing the vacant chair for Banquo. The disorder with which the scene closed was marked by the noisy upturning of tables and chairs; the disarray much at odds with the opening formality.

THE SIGNIFICANCE OF THE THREE SETTINGS

These three very distinctive productions provide very good examples of the way that scenery or setting can suggest an interpretation of a play to the audience. No textual evidence supported the ecclesiastical setting of 1974. The black magic circle of 1976 originated from the transfer of the 1974 production to London when much of the church furniture was abandoned and the circle used instead. It became the principal focus for The Other Place production. The title page of Christopher Marlowe's *Dr Faustus* (Quarto edition, 1624) showed the Doctor standing in a similar circle as he conjured the devilish form of Mephostophilis.

The structure of the 1982 production had two elements that remind us of the Globe Theatre in which many of Shakespeare's plays were performed. First there was the thrust, or apron stage, with the audience sitting round three of its sides. Then there was the scaffolding platform which was not unlike the gallery that overlooked the apron stage of the Elizabethan playhouse.

Essentially each of these settings developed out of the director's interpretation of the play. Trevor Nunn's first production immediately gave the play a religious dimension, the struggle between Good and Evil, God and the Devil, a saintly Duncan against a satanic Macbeth. The same director's second production suggested a much more personal compact between Macbeth and the Devil through the agency of the Witches—the bargain was sealed within that circle apparently magic in its power. There was no magic or religion in Howard Davies' 1982 production. For him, the tragedy concerned the hazards of political advancement in a country controlled by a military government. The set itself was hard-edged, stark, uncompromising—a reflection of that society where aggressiveness ruled.

It was interesting to note that though the settings were so different the costume designs for all three productions had much in common. Few allusions were made to Scotland or Scottish national costume. Instead, each director preferred to emphasise the military, soldierly aspects of the characters. Costumes for the most part consisted of brass-buttoned greatcoats, leather jackets, serge collarless tunics, heavy belts and holsters and jackboots. The women's costumes afforded little relief. A white dress, a gold circlet or a fur coat, briefly assumed for the coronation were the only adornments of the otherwise sombre Lady Macbeth costumes. Grey/black raggedness was the characteristic of all the Witches. The dominant tones of black, grey or dull red contributed powerfully to an overall impression of a dour, harsh, serious world of callous murder, betrayal and retribution. . . .

STAGING THE WITCHES

The particular function and influence that the Witches have on Macbeth's decisions has been a subject of frequent debate. Performance adds another complication concerning their physical appearance. An illustration in the 1587 edition of Holinshed's *Chronicle* shows three upright, smartly dressed bonneted ladies confronting Macbeth and Banquo dressed as Elizabethan gentlemen. There is no suggestion of the bearded hags that Banquo describes. His observation is very precise:

> You seem to understand me,
> By each at once her choppy finger laying
> Upon her skinny lips. You should be women,
> And yet your beards forbid me to interpret
> That you are so.
>
> (1.3.43-7)

When Macbeth visits their cavern, the Witches are concocting in their cauldron a magic potion made of villainous ingredients and they are able to conjure a series of apparitions as well as displaying a Show of Kings. Their appearances, though brief, are visually spectacular. Their presence in the play offers complexities of characterisation, presentation and interpretation. Each production sought a different solution.

In 1974, the director saw the Witches representing the reverse side of the specifically Christian imagery that the church setting presented. After the coronation of Duncan they invaded the sacred space, riding the chandelier as if it were their own space vehicle. Their coarse, torn shapeless garments made them ugly earth creatures as they squatted round their open bundle containing the instruments and vessels of the black mass. One critic noted: 'The Weird Sisters . . . gave Macbeth and Banquo a drugged posset when they met them on the blasted hearth rug.' The apparitions were small mis-shapen puppets and the line of kings was seen only by Macbeth. The whole effect was of ugly chanting women, gross priestesses of black magic, absorbed in their degraded rites that mocked Christianity. They exerted a hypnotic attraction for Macbeth who failed to recognise them as 'instruments of darkness.'

The black magic circle in 1976 provided the natural habitat for the Witches. The world it contained was their domain. Again their costumes were crude, tattered garments of coarse wool and moulting fur. Their voices at one moment were snarling, shrieking cries, at another whispered, chilling moans. Of Macbeth's visit to the Witches in this production, Richard David wrote:

> The witches' cavern exhibited no marvels, no doom-long line of kings. On entering, Macbeth was seized by the witches, his back stripped and branded with sooty cabalistic[3] symbols. The three 'voices' were spoken by the witches as they held up in turn three horrible wizened emblems which were thereafter kept clutched in Macbeth's hands till the ineffectiveness of one talisman after another had been demonstrated. For the show of Banquo's royal issue his eyes were blindfolded and the vision was an internal one. (*Shakespeare in the Theatre* p. 87)

Their evil was pervasive. Their voices echoed everywhere. They crouched sometimes visible, sometimes unseen, a dark ever-present menace.

There were no bearded chins or choppy fingers in 1982. These Witches, three beautiful, young be-jeaned or skirted women in tie-dye blouses of pastel pink and blues immediately gathered up strewn lengths of dull grey fabric which they wound round their bodies to distort or deform their shapes. These actions were accompanied by a discordant disjointed recital of the opening lines, garbled, repeated, tossed from one to another. These chanting, half-mad, yet beautiful women immediately introduced a sense of disorder with their broken language and unexpected actions.

No cauldron was to be expected and none appeared. The Show of Kings was represented by the physical presence of the figures of Duncan, Banquo and their families solidly displaying the royal succession. The group, standing motionless, seemed to fill the stage beyond the shutter-like doors.

These Weird Sisters had none of the attributes nor performed any action that might traditionally have been associated with Shakespeare's Witches. The disorder that these represented was created by the curious and violent contrast between their appearance and their speech. Their physical beauty was immediately distorted, their language, attractive in utterance, broke into almost impenetrable confusion. Such uneasy and disturbed women were best kept at a distance.

DIFFERENT DETAILS, COMMON PURPOSE

The characterisation of the Witches in 1976 developed from the 1974 production. For example, the idea of making the third Witch a twitching, deformed creature was retained.

---

3. having a secret or hidden meaning; occult

The Witches were women, but always crouching, earth-bound creatures in a sordid, unkempt world. They displayed an intense possessiveness over their ugly shrunken puppets or crude talismen. Their language was made up of discordant shrieking, whispers, moans and cries. Physical and vocal abnormality proclaimed them as inhabitants of a Witch-world with grossly evil intentions. At first they provoked wary curiosity in Macbeth and Banquo, but it was Macbeth who overcame the physical repulsion, drawn by the secrets they seemed to hold.

In striking contrast there was nothing obviously witchlike in the characters in the third production. This apparent absence of evil deceived Macbeth. As a seasoned man of the world, he was sure that he could handle this unusual, but no doubt tractable, trio. His inability to recognise their evil and his willingness to seek further guidance from them demonstrated a lack of judgment not to be expected in an experienced soldier and politician. So, as surely as the Witches in the earlier productions, these strange young women encouraged Macbeth in his ambitions and through their misleading information precipitated his final downfall.

Macbeth's Rich Visual Effects

D.J. Palmer

D.J. Palmer's analysis of *Macbeth* shows that the language and imagery of the play offer audiences a rich visual spectacle. Palmer interprets recurring events and settings, visually dramatic entrances and exits, and reported but unseen events. D.J. Palmer has taught English at the University of Manchester in England and served as general editor of *Stratford-upon-Avon Studies.* He is a frequent contributor to *Critical Quarterly* and *Shakespeare Survey.*

The faculty of sight has special significance in *Macbeth.* Not only do 'sightless substances' assume visible shape and bloody spectacles appal us, but we are made as aware of what is veiled from our eyes (for instance, the murder of Duncan) as of what is seen. There are degrees of visibility, and the language of the play, with its powerful appeal to the visual imagination, mediates between the seen and the unseen. The inner world of Macbeth's visionary awareness, expressed through his soliloquies, and the off-stage world reported by the play's many messengers, contain images that extend the play's concern with sight beyond what is visible on the stage. This verbal imagery and the recurrent references to the eye itself as a vulnerable agent, prone to deception and confronted by what it hardly dare look upon, add the power of suggestion to the play's visual impact.

RECURRING SCENES AND SETTINGS

Just as the linguistic structure of *Macbeth* contains ironic repetitions and reiterative patterns of imagery, so too does its use of spectacle. There are visual as well as verbal echoes, creating dramatic meaning through parallels and contrasts. For instance, the play begins and ends in battle, al-

Reprinted from D.J. Palmer, " 'A New Gorgon': Visual Effects in *Macbeth*," in *Focus On Macbeth,* edited by John Russell Brown (London: Routledge, 1982) by permission of the publisher.

though only in the final battle does fighting take place on the stage. At the beginning, the stage-image of Duncan 'in his great office' takes precedence over the actual sound and fury of battle, as, attended by the princes and nobles, he receives news of the defeated rebels and dispenses honours to his loyal thanes. The bleeding Captain, the first of the play's messengers and the first of its sanguinary figures, is a sight, like the tale he tells, more heroic than horrific. There is a distinction between blood shed in a just cause and murder, and an ironic recapitulation of this image of the wounded Captain reporting to his King occurs when the First Murderer is seen informing Macbeth of Banquo's death ('There's blood upon thy face.' 'Tis Banquo's then,' III.iv.13), a point which gains emphasis if Macbeth in the later scene is wearing the royal insignia first worn by Duncan. The final climactic battle is more spectacular than the first. We see the drums and colours of the opposing forces, and instead of the bleeding Captain's news of the rebels' defeat, a messenger brings word to Macbeth that Birnam Wood is moving towards Dunsinane. As battle is joined, a rapid sequence of entries and exits and stage-combats culminates in the image of the victorious Malcolm, attended by the same nobles who were seen with his father in the play's opening scenes, with Macbeth's severed head (on a pole, according to Holinshed) visually recalling the justice formerly executed by Macbeth himself on the traitor Macdonwald.

The outdoor location of these opening and concluding scenes is dramatically significant and should be visually apparent. The action of the play moves from battlefield and heath into the confines of Macbeth's castle, as evil closes in. Lady Macbeth's first appearance, alone, is the first scene set indoors, and as she takes charge of the stage she also takes charge of the impending situation. Far from suggesting security, the sense of moving into an interior world is that of oppressive confinement, or sometimes of violent intrusion. The cave in which Macbeth confronts the 'secret, black and midnight hags' is therefore a stage-image of particular significance (Hecate refers to it as 'the pit of Acheron', III.v.15). The movement from these dark, enclosed worlds out into the open again in the final scenes is liberating and restorative.

Another pattern of visual repetition is formed by the two feasts in the play. Macbeth is host on both occasions, but the first, in honour of Duncan, takes place off-stage and is represented only by the processional entry at the opening of I.vii: 'Hautboys,torches. Enter a *Sewer*, and divers *Servants* with dishes and service over the stage.' This brief pageant, both functional and emblematic, serves to express the festive values of fellowship and community which Macbeth will destroy, and indeed no sooner has the procession passed over the stage than Macbeth enters to meditate on 'the horrid deed'. Its sequel is the coronation feast in III.iv, another travesty of social concord, as the ghost of the murdered Banquo makes its unwelcome appearance. The interrupted feast, with the guests departing in confusion and disarray, spectacularly confirms the words of Lady Macbeth: 'the sauce to meat is ceremony; / Meeting were bare without it' (III.iv. 36–7).

CONTRASTS AND ECHOES IN THE WITCHES' SCENES

An ironic visual counterpart to this feast, with its spectral visitation, is the Cauldron Scene, of which G. Wilson Knight has written [in *The Imperial Theme*], 'Here we watch a devil's banqueting, the Weird Women with their cauldron and its hideous ingredients. The banquet idea has been inverted.' This scene is the climactic point of the play's use of spectacle: the cauldron itself is an image traditionally associated with hell, and each of the three Apparitions in turn rises and descends from within it. The presentation of these sights by the witches to Macbeth is a diabolical parody of the emblematic pageants and allegorical masques with which royalty was greeted and honoured in Shakespeare's day, often at a banquet. Like the shows in such court entertainments, each of the Apparitions directly addresses the principal guest, offering counsel and flattering assurance. On this occasion, however, the Apparitions take the shapes that Macbeth should fear most: the traitor's severed head, the babe 'from his mother's womb / Untimely ripp'd' and the lineal heir to the crown who bears the tree from Birnam Wood to Dunsinane. This is followed by a sight which does appal Macbeth but which ironically incorporates what is a complimentary allusion from the point of view of a Jacobean audience: 'A Show of eight *Kings*, and *Banquo* last; the last king with a glass in his hand.' This tribute to the ancestry of King James with its implication that his line will last for ever is in keeping with the usual function of this kind of spectacle. The 'entertainment' is completed with the witches' 'antic round'. . . .

As Macbeth's second encounter with the witches, the Cauldron Scene echoes their first meeting on the heath only to emphasise the differences. Instead of being accosted by the witches, and betraying fear at their words, it is now Macbeth who seeks them out, aggressively demanding to know the worst. Prophecy now takes visible shape, and the general effect of the contrast is to suggest an intensification of evil. Whoever was responsible for the introduction of Hecate,[1] the scene in which she first appears, III.v, balances the play's opening scene as each [witch] prepares for an encounter with Macbeth. The addition of Hecate is in keeping with the hellish associations of the cave and cauldron, and with the sense that we are closer here than at the beginning of the play to spirits of greater power than the witches themselves. Moreover, although modern editors provide Hecate with an exit before Macbeth's entry in the Cauldron Scene, the First Folio does not. Her presence is not essential and she does not speak after Macbeth has entered, but as a presiding figure, visible to the audience though unseen by Macbeth (as the Ghost of Banquo in the feast scene appears to Macbeth but not to the other characters), she would add to the spectacular as well as the ironic effects of the scene. Hecate, after all, is a goddess, not a grotesque hag, and a spectral counterpart to that other Queen of Night, Lady Macbeth.

A catalogue of all the visual echoes in the play would also include the two Doctors, the English doctor who describes the miraculous powers of healing possessed by the saintly Edward the Confessor, and his counterpart, the Doctor who in the following scene looks on with the Gentlewoman as Lady Macbeth sleep-walks: 'More needs she the divine than the physician' (V.i.72). Lady Macbeth's sleep-walking is itself a visual and verbal repetition, a re-enactment of former sights and acts. The compulsive rubbing of her hand, for instance, ironically recalls her words after the murder of Duncan, 'A little water clears us of this deed' (II.ii.67). In her trancelike state, with her open but expressionless eyes, she creates a visual effect more like that of a ghost than of a living woman. . . .

THE SPECTACLE OF ENTRANCES AND EXITS

Many of the play's entries and exits are visually expressive moments. Exactly how characters should arrive and depart,

---

1. In Greek mythology Hecate is an ancient fertility goddess who later becomes associated with Persephone as queen of Hades and protector of witches.

and how those they join or leave should react, are matters for the director and players to discover. But the context often strongly suggests that such moments create significant stage-images. I have already referred to the explicit comment on the 'haste' with which Ross enters in I.ii, and many of the play's numerous other messengers will bring their news similar urgency, breaking unexpectedly upon the scene. The First Murderer who reports Banquo's death to Macbeth in III.iv is given a mere 'Enter' in the Folio stage-direction, but in 1767 Edward Capell added 'to the door', a phrase which has been adopted by most subsequent editors of the play and which indicates how furtively he appears and waits at the door until Macbeth crosses to him. This 'door' itself might acquire powerful visual associations if it is also that through which Macbeth leaves to murder Duncan ('as his host, / Who should against his murderer shut the door, / Not bear the knife myself,' I.vii.14–16), through which he re-enters after the murder, and to which he leads Macduff ('This is the door,' II.iii.49) after the latter and Lennox have been admitted by the Porter. Another entrance must serve as the 'south entry', which the Porter likens to 'hell-gate', and it might be this which is later used by the Ghost of Banquo and by Macbeth in the Cauldron Scene, where his entry-cue is the Second Witch's line, 'Open, locks, whoever knocks' (IV.i.46).

To conclude each of Macbeth's two encounters with them, the witches 'Vanish', according to the Folio stage-direction. This presumably indicates the use of the trap, through which the cauldron and the three Apparitions also rise and descend. However it is managed, the disappearance of the witches is an exit startling enough to draw astonished comment from Macbeth and Banquo and one that visibly, or perhaps invisibly, demonstrates their unnatural powers. Equally ingenious is the first entry of the Ghost of Banquo in the Feast Scene, though in this case the ingenuity is one of timing rather than stage-machinery. By having the Ghost enter several lines before it is seen by Macbeth, Shakespeare heightens the audience's horrified anticipation and ironic awareness. Its appearance to the audience, followed by Macbeth's delayed recognition and the inability of the other characters to see it, is a visual arrangement which conveys a sense of the spectral as much as the ghastly figure itself. . . .

Entries and exits register strong impressions in the scenes immediately before and after the murder of Duncan.

After the brilliant festive torches borne in the processional entries of I.vi and vii, the single torch held by Fleance as he and Banquo open II.i is a puny light, insufficient for them to recognise Macbeth as he approaches, himself attended by a torch-bearer. These single torches, like that which Fleance carries again on his entrance with his father in III.iii, do not merely inform us that night has fallen; they suggest what little protection there is against the forces of darkness. Indeed, in the latter scene, it is the light of the torch which betrays Banquo to his murderers and Fleance escapes when it is extinguished. (In the Sleep-walking Scene, the taper held by Lady Macbeth, although she sees nothing, is a visual echo that emphasises the pathos of her appearance, a 'brief candle' guttering in the dark.) To revert to II.i, the departure of Banquo and Fleance followed shortly by Macbeth's dismissal of his servant, takes the torches off and leaves Macbeth alone, more intensely alone than if he had entered an empty stage to wait for the bell that is his cue for murder. His exit after his soliloquy concludes the scene on the highest pitch of tension so far reached in the play.

The entry of Lady Macbeth which follows sustains that tension, for there is evidently no break in the time-sequence and her words make us aware of the proximity of the murder off-stage. Macbeth's re-entry, therefore, must be a stunning sight. . . . However the entry is made, with whatever motion and expression the actor feels to be right, it will be to create an appalled and appalling sight. This is a changed Macbeth, but there need be no change in his appearance except that which can be expressed by the actor's face and body. It is not until six lines after his entry that Macbeth speaks of the 'sorry sight' of his bloody hands, and the delayed revelation of that spectacle, as he unclenches his fists that still grasp the daggers, is another concentrated visual effect. The hasty exit of the couple, prompted by the insistent knocking at the gate, requires Lady Macbeth virtually to take her stupefied husband from the scene. Her words in the Sleep-walking Scene, 'Come, come, come, come, give me your hand' (V.i.65), suggest an appropriate action to convey in their exit an image of their partnership sealed in blood.

The discovery of the murder precipitates a rapid sequence of entries and exits, generating an effect of confusion, shock and suspicion. Macduff, who proclaims the dreadful fact (visually, his entry as from Duncan's chamber is part of the pattern of messengers bringing urgent news), also takes immediate charge of the situation; his prominence in this scene first establishes his importance in the play. Apart from Macduff and Lennox, the characters appear in night-attire, roused by the alarum bell. Banquo's words, 'When we have our naked frailties hid, / That suffer in exposure, let us meet' (II.iii.125–6), not only give the textual indication of this but voice as well the sense of vulnerability and unpreparedness which their state of undress depicts. The murder of Duncan leaves them all insecure.

There are other entries and exits later in the play, not so far mentioned, of strong visual impact and significance. For instance, only a few lines after Macduff's grimly ironic farewell to Banquo, 'Adieu, / Lest our old robes sit easier than our new' (II.iv.37–8), there occurs in the following scene the entry of the coronation procession, in which Macbeth wears the borrowed robes of majesty. After enquiring of Banquo what his movements are to be before supper, Macbeth dismisses everyone except a Servant; the Folio's stage-direction, 'Exeunt *Lords*', obscures the fact that Lady Macbeth also withdraws at his injunction. In performance, however, her exclusion from his company makes her exit striking evidence of the change in their relationship. Without her knowledge, he now plots the killing of Banquo with the two Murderers, so that when he enters to her in the next scene, their rejoining is heavily underscored by the unwitting irony of her solicitous greeting, 'How now, my lord! Why do you keep alone, / Of sorriest fancies your companions making' (III.ii.8–9). . . .

There is one other entry which must not be overlooked in this survey, if only because it creates a visual effect quite different from the prevailing concern with horror and fear. This is the appearance at the beginning of V.vi of Malcolm and his army with their 'leavy screens'. What is to Malcolm a tactical device for disguising the strength of his forces, and to Macbeth the scarcely credible fulfilment of the prophecy of a seemingly impossible event, appears to the audience to identify Malcolm's army with the reassertion of the natural order, as if the land itself has risen against Macbeth. It is an emblematic tableau, yet another instance of a visual image drawing its expressive value from the play's verbal imagery of growth and fertility, and it endows Malcolm's cause and that of Macduff with more than personal significance.

THE POWER OF UNSEEN EVENTS

An audience can be made as conscious of not seeing something of dramatic importance as it is of what it actually witnesses, and in this respect *Macbeth* is as remarkable for its unstaged events as for its many sensational sights. . . .

The deaths of Lady Macbeth and Macbeth are both offstage events. The Sleep-walking Scene prepares us for the end of Lady Macbeth: she concludes her part on the stage, as she began it, alone, despite the presence of the Doctor and the Gentlewoman. By not staging her death, Shakespeare makes it a reported event to which Macbeth reacts with a speech of sombre gravity but without any sense of personal loss or grief; since we do not see it, we are also open to Malcolm's suggestion at the end of the play that she took her own life. Macbeth's own death is also obscured from our view, despite the stage-direction of the Folio, 'Enter Fighting, and *Macbeth* slaine.' This stage-direction might be taken to indicate that Macbeth is seen to receive a fatal wound in his fight with Macduff, but he does not die on the stage. . . . Our last image of Macbeth alive is appropriately that of a man fighting against the odds, and the sight of Macbeth's head brought in by Macduff is a fitting conclusion to the play's visual horrors.

The Role of the Porter

Marvin Rosenberg

Marvin Rosenberg analyzes the Porter's role, detailing the dress, movements, and interruptions required of an actor who must stall and give Macbeth and Lady Macbeth sufficient time to clean up after the murder of Duncan. Rosenberg also elaborates on two characters that enter the Porter's imaginary hell, the significance of an opened door, and the meaning of time. Marvin Rosenberg teaches drama at the University of California at Berkeley and is the author of *The Masks of Othello, The Masks of King Lear, The Masks of Macbeth,* and *The Adventures of a Shakespeare Scholar.*

Enter a Porter. Knocking within.

The man shambling across the stage is going to open the great castle door, sometimes apparent at the far end of the great courtyard—in the Globe, perhaps at one of the wing entrances—but he must move slowly to do it. As Capell[1] long ago recognized, Macbeth must have time to change and wash his hands. . . . The Porter interlude serves importantly, also, to stretch the felt time between the preceding murder scene and what is to come by mocking the actual clock-time with fairest show; but of this more later.

Shakespeare makes a blessing of the necessity of hiatus: using the sound of knocking for a bridge, he begins to bring some faint light into the dark castle, to break for a moment the terrible grip of the murder scene. The knocking signals the awakening of the outer world, as De Quincey sensed; but the outside is allowed in only by a marvelously contrived intermediacy: this sleepy, drunken Porter. At once visually, and in his succeeding language and action, he exploits central motifs in the play. . . .

---

1. Rosenberg, the author of this essay, refers to a variety of critics, directors, and actors by last name only.

Excerpted from Marvin Rosenberg, *The Masks of Macbeth* (Berkeley and Los Angeles: University of California Press, 1978). Reprinted by permission of the author.

The Porter's character easily authenticates his delay in opening his doors. He has taken full advantage of the great celebration the night before. Like the king, he has been in unusual pleasure. Granville-Barker takes some pains to rescue the Porter from candidacy in an "inebriates home"—but this door keeper has certainly drunk his fill. He sometimes hiccups or belches when he speaks. He stumbles on, nursing his hangover, perhaps trying even now to cure it with more of what gave it to him. . . .

The Porter bridges us from one moment of tragedy to another, never letting us escape the implications of a murderous world he inhabits, yet dressing them in the rough, humorous language and action of inspired earthy foolery. The actor who played the part for Shakespeare may not have said more than was set down for him—though part of that might have been at his suggestion; he almost certainly "played" more than the Folio sets down, as his comic physical invention thrived; and so have succeeding Porters. . . .

His very appearance is a kind of joke: his below-stairs dress—or undress; his earthiness—he is of the earth, as the Sisters are of the air; his functional, sometimes coarse, movement. He has been played as an old, old retainer; as a sinister, toad-like cripple; as a pure Clown figure; as a kind of comic devil who rises from the trap; but he serves best as a "common man," enclosing a choral voice on the follies of mankind in a dramatic identity too distinctive to be quite Anyman's.

THE PORTER FILLS TIME AND CREATES HUMOR

His jesting does not stand by itself; it accompanies his fuddled attempts to get to that door, and open it. The action line must not suffer: a murder has been committed, and may momentarily be exposed. . . .

He must get onto the stage first of all. Craig had him rolling out in his sack bed. From such an obstacle he has to struggle; he can comment on the knocking as he does so. Or he stumbles out, half-blind with sleep and drink, half-dressed, and must throw his clothes on. He tries to move while arranging a kilt, or pulling up his trousers—an immemorial comic action. He may never quite get them right. . . .

Then he has to orient himself. He staggers, groping in the dark. If a fire burns in the courtyard, as with Tree, he must try to kick it up, warm himself. He will need a lantern. He must find it; perhaps even light it, if it is not hanging lit. He may be too drunk to find at once the wall where the door is, and feel for it.

Against the wall, his back to us, he may pause to urinate. This seems a universal device for delay: it has been used by Porters in Japan, in Czechoslovakia, in the Polanski film.

After the lantern, he may have to find a key. This is likely to be a large key, and may elude his search for a good part of a speech, until he finds it—perhaps tied around his neck or waist. Having found the key, he must still locate the door. If instead of a keyed door he must turn a winch to lift a gate, he can expend a good deal of his imaginary dialogue finding the mechanism, fitting the handle, and pulling at it. Meanwhile, the knocking may hurt his hungover head, even seem to sound inside it; he may put his hands over his ears, wincing at each rap; may shush the sound.

THE PORTER PLAYS HELL'S GATEKEEPER, USHERING IN CANDIDATES

These are typical large movements. They help provide a spine for his progress to the door, but must never interfere with his dialogue, which comes when his efforts to advance, or get the door open, are interrupted by the knocking. His first lines, usually from across the stage as he starts his sleepy, yawning, long journey to the door, tell his grumbling, ironic mood.

> Here's a knocking indeed: if a man
> were Porter of Hell-gate, he should
> have old turning the key—
>
> (4–6)

so many come in.

Shakespeare excels at blur and irony. The Porter is a player, like his betters; talks to imaginary figures, like his betters; fits his behavior to a cosmic frame, like his betters. Murder has been committed in a castle where "Heaven's breath smells wooingly." The place where gentle birds procreate is a scene of violent death. God will be called upon, and keep silence. They who knock at the door have their own faults—the two live thanes, and the Porter's imaginary visitors. It is a complex world.

The Porter's hell-guests belong to the times. The farmer's suicide from producing too much may reflect the steep drop in English prices in 1605–1606. Typical topical pornographic allusions have been scented in all the Porter says, beginning with "sweat" in *you'll sweat for't.* Harcourt relates this to the sweat-tub therapy for venereal disease. . . .

Porters have had various ways of ushering their candidates into hell. One mock-bows them in, one beckons with a finger, another makes a grand, courtly, Osric-type sweep; another kicks their backsides as they are imagined entering, another prods with a handy pitchfork, real or mimed. One Porter spoke to little bugs he held up after discovering them on the door, as he tried to fit his key to the lock. . . .

THE EQUIVOCATOR AND ROBBER ARE SIGNIFICANT TO THE PLAY

The Porter hardly gets one "guest" in when the knocking, always louder, more insistent, nudges him toward opening the door—and sometimes toward fortifying himself again from a bottle. He mimics the knock sound, often with a kind of resentful good humor; this is part of the play he is acting. Bernard Dukore remembers one who played with the word itself: "ka-nock, ka-nock."

Now the Equivocator is passed in (and the Porter may, by juggling hands as if balancing weights, image the play's ticklish equilibriums):

> that could swear in both the scales against either scale, who committed treason enough for God's sake, yet could not equivocate to heaven: oh come in, Equivocator.
>
> (11-14)

The implication for the character of Macbeth and for the action of the play needs no explication. The play begins and ends with treason: "bad" treason, and good. For the Jacobeans, this Equivocator was also, apparently a Jesuitical figure who could evade, in the name of his religion, a truthful answer to a political question. Danks argues that resentment was directed against Equivocators generally (he cites the horrible mutilation and execution of the first Jesuit martyr in England); as Muir and others have observed from the evidence, Shakespeare seems to have meant specifically the Father Garnet who was involved in the "Gunpowder Plot" to blow up parliament and the king. . . .

Such deliberate misleading is only one of the kinds of equivocation in *Macbeth.* Macbeth and Lady Macbeth will say and act one thing when they mean another; so will others: thus Lenox to the Lord in III, vi and Malcolm to Macduff in IV, i. The Sisters,

HELL'S GATEKEEPER

Though stage directions in act 2, scene 2 say simply, "Enter a Porter," he enters with an array of comic gestures and a monologue with himself as the imaginary porter to hell's gate.

Enter a PORTER. *Knocking within.*

PORTER. Here's a knocking indeed! If a man were porter of hell gate, he should have old[1] turning the key. [*Knock.*] Knock, knock, knock! Who's there, i' th' name of Belzebub? Here's a farmer that hang'd himself on th' expectation of plenty.[2] Come in time! Have napkins[3] enow about you; here you'll sweat for't. [*Knock.*] Knock, knock! Who's there, in the' other devil's name? Faith, here's an equivocator,[4] that could swear in both the scales against either scale; who committed treason enough for God's sake, yet could not equivocate to heaven. O, come in, equivocator! [*Knock.*] Knock, knock, knock! Who's there? Faith, here's an English tailor come hither for stealing out of a French hose.[5] Come in tailor. Here you may roast your goose.[6] [*Knock.*] Knock, knock! Never at quiet! What are you? But this place is too cold for hell. I'll devil-porter it no further. I had thought to have let in some of all professions that go the primrose way to th'everlasting bonfire. [*Knock.*] Anon, anon! [*Opens the gate.*] I pray you remember the porter.

1. **old:** slang for "any amount of" 2. **farmer . . . plenty:** Farmers hoarded in times of plenty hoping for high prices in times of shortage. One farmer hanged himself when he failed to profit. When his neighbors cut him down, he abuses them for not untying the rope. 3. **napkins:** towels 4. **equivocator:** a reference to the trial and execution of Father Garnet for being an accessory to the Gunpowder Plot. 5. **English . . . hose:** a double theft: he stole the fashion and some cloth, for French hose were full and baggy 6. **goose:** a pun on goose, the tailor's pressing iron

as we have seen, practice equivocation more ambiguously: they mean more than they say to Macbeth, but we must wonder if it is they, or Hecate, or their masters, or life itself, or any of its mysterious forces, finally responsible for paltering with him in a double sense. Shakespeare, the creator of all this uncertainty, is himself the Great Equivocator, punning, doubling images and ideas, shifting perspectives on characters and motifs, pointing action in a direction it does not go. Aptly, the playwright uses only in *Macbeth* the words *equivocate, equivocates,* and *equivocator*; the play shares with *Hamlet* alone *equivocation.*

The Porter scene reflects—almost, with this second hellbound figure, stipulates—the motif of equivocation weaving through the play: the doubling of voices, attitudes, images in opposition, or—in Stirling's words—in contradiction. This style and substance validates the scene as Shakespeare's, Muir observes:

> It possesses the antithetical characteristics of the verse, transposed for semi-comic purposes. The whole scene is linked so closely with the rest of the play, in content as well as style. . . . The antithetical style is a powerful means of suggesting the paradox and enigma of the nature of man.

The Porter's next guest is a robber—and possibly here, too, Macbeth the throne-thief is faintly paralleled.

> Faith here's an English Tailor come hither,
> for stealing out of a French hose.
>
> (15-16)

This seems to be a joke against the English for the English to laugh at, like the Gravedigger's joke about a mad Hamlet not being noticed in a land full of English madmen. . . .

THE PORTER OPENS THE DOOR TO TWO THANES AND MORE

The Porter dissolves his illusion of hell. The bonfire is as imaginary as the guests, the place is too cold; and he has reached the door, turned the key, slid the bolt, winched the gate, whatever—and the knocking is now peremptory. *Anon, anon.* He had thought to let in some of all professions, he says—often pausing to look significantly at the audience. He does, at last, open to the two thanes—with a gesture, overt or behind their backs, that repeats his ushering of his imaginary guests. But in this real world he remembers to say, with open palm or proffered cap:

> I pray you remember the Porter.
>
> (22)

Hall's sardonic devil-porter let his gaze swing to include the audience, and the line was said more meaningfully to the house than to the other actors. All, all were guests in his hell.

The great door, opening, lets in the two men, and more. The sodden atmosphere emanating from the Porter, following on the nightmare climate of the murder scene, has thickened and soiled the air. It freshens with the entrance of two brisk thanes, the sense of the outside world they bring with them, and perhaps a breeze—the Porter's lantern has been seen blown out in modern productions, and may have been at the Globe. Or there the signs of dawn could have been understood when the complaint was made of the Porter's late lying, and he put his torch out; controlled lighting in later productions specifies it.

The opening of doors on a closed, secret place, and the letting in of light and fresh men, impart a symbolic as well as realistic effect. New life has the chance to enter—as, in other circumstances, given silence and outer darkness, death may be associated with an open portal. A psychologist suggests that the knocking to enter symbolizes the awakening of the self-preserving conscious part of the mind to relief from the murderous demands of the id. The passing of the night itself brings an archetypal relief.

Shakespeare, daring to charge his Porter with lying late, again whirls us through time by his compressive art. Various kinds of time serve him. First is measured time, with its varieties: the given time of night and day of the play, and the references to the actual clock time taken by the play's incidents. Sometimes opposed to this is the time *felt* as passing by the spectator. Our sense of clock time is generally suspended with our disbelief, as long as it is not challenged by absurdity. Shakespeare risks the limits: Banquo has said goodnight to Macbeth about midnight, Macbeth goes swiftly to murder Duncan, Lady Macbeth comes urgently to extricate him from the sequel, and at once a knocking is heard heralding, in performance time, the morn. In the murder and post-murder scenes the *felt* passage of time is unmeasured: we experience an agony that stretches out toward doom. This experience dissolves into the Porter's scene; and, as suggested above, one important function of that scene is to hoodwink the time, to cushion our return to the intrusion—in performance time hours later—of the outside world.

Another kind of time we are exposed to is experienced as abstract, measureless: it is the now, or, alternatively, it is eternity—the two concepts of time that had to be considered in Macbeth's I, vii soliloquy. As we are absorbed in the sequence of nows, on momentary banks and shoals of time, we can be transported from one to the other without questioning—as long as the playwright's art strings them into a linear flow that sustains illusion. Often the now in *Macbeth* takes place in the shadow of eternity; the Porter, as immediate as earth, yet involves us in awareness of the life beyond life, in his comic way; as Macbeth has involved us in the universe of time and space in his sterner introspections—those contextual moments when action is temporarily subordinated to an exploration of the human condition.

CHAPTER 3

Shakespeare's Technique and Craft

READINGS ON
MACBETH

Macbeth: An Atypical Tragedy

Clifford Davidson

Clifford Davidson discusses *Macbeth* as tragedy, not according to Aristotle's definition, but according to the cultural and religious beliefs of Shakespeare's time. Davidson argues that hypocrisy is Macbeth's sin, which deprives him of sensitivity and makes him a tyrant guilty of great wrongs. Rather than feeling pity and goodwill for the protagonist at the end, the alienated audience judges Macbeth and regrets only that he has lost all goodness. Clifford Davidson has taught at Western Michigan University in Kalamazoo. He is the author of a collection of poems, *The Thirsting Seer,* editor of *Universitas: A Journal of Religion and the University,* and frequent contributor to the *Journal of Aesthetics and Art Criticism* and other scholarly journals.

The road which Macbeth travels "to dusty death" involves him in hypocrisy and deception, which are confirmed by the treason he commits. He is unable to appear in public without the mask which he is forced to wear in order that he might conceal the malice of his heart. He appears to Duncan as an angel of light; inwardly, he is a ravening wolf in the service of darkness. Duncan, "a most Sainted-King" (IV, iii, 125), is deceived by Macbeth's show of holiness but, once the initial crime is completed, the usurper's nature becomes progressively known through his acts. As the Bible (*Matthew* vii, 10) and the *Homilies*[1] proclaim, men must be judged "by their fruits." Immediately after the murder of the king, Macduff and Banquo suspect, but in III, vi Lennox and another lord know more exactly the nature of Macbeth's cunning. Hypocrisy is not able to cover itself entirely with pretended sanctity. . . .

1. Two Books of Homilies, first published in 1547 and 1563, were appointed to be read from the pulpits of the Church of England.

Reprinted from Clifford Davidson, *The Primrose Way: A Study of Shakespeare's* Macbeth (Conesville, IA: John Westburg & Associates, 1970), by permission of the author. Copyright 1970 by John Edward Westburg.

91

The final devilish state of Macbeth's soul is not to be judged from his beginning, which appears to be good, but from his end. Once caught by the devil's bait, only at the end is he able to express his inward state openly in outward appearance. By Act V, Macbeth has become a stereotyped stage tyrant who is unashamedly malicious. . . .

Faced with the judgment which Malcolm's soldiers will work against him, Macbeth has little choice except to fight: "Bear-like I must fight the course" (V, vii, 4). His hypocritical behavior has reduced him to the level of bestiality, and now he must die like a beast. Edward Philips[2] admonishes his auditory: "learn . . . what an abominable thing sin is, and among the rest hypocrisy, that it is able to transform men into beasts, as resembling them in their qualities." Sin does change Macbeth strangely so that all his former nobility is destroyed or changed into something sub-human. In V, viii, 6, Macduff appropriately calls Macbeth a "hell-hound.". . .

MACBETH MAKES A MOCKERY OF THE CROWN AND THE KINGLY ROBES

Macbeth's hope and desire to gain the coveted symbol of kingship similarly turn out to be a mockery. If he must sell his eternal jewel to gain an earthly crown, he thereby is frustrating any hope his soul might have of gaining a heavenly crown. And because of the position of the king in the hierarchy, the wearing of the earthly crown by Macbeth can only be a mockery. Only one who shares heavenly hope has the right to reach for the symbolic crown.

Like the crown, the kingly robes which Macbeth wears after the completion of Act II are symbols of kingly authority and position. As symbols, they appear to participate in the sanctity of the office which they represent. . . . The outward sign is abused when it is not consistent with the inner reality. In this case, the sign—Macbeth's royal robes—are symbolic of authority and dominion which do not in fact exist. The clothing of the hypocrite is of much greater value than his own worth.

The clothes imagery in *Macbeth* therefore ought to be seen as underlining the theme of hypocrisy in the play. In I, iii, Ross's announcement of Macbeth's new honor and position as Thane of Cawdor is greeted with a question: "Why do you

2. rector of Saint Saviors in Southwark, published *Certain Godly and Learned Sermons* in 1604

dress me in borrowed robes?" Soon, however, Macbeth will attempt to dress himself in the hope of wearing the crown and kingly robes which rightly belong to Duncan. As things turn out, the Macbeth who dons those kingly garments demonstrates that he is only "a dwarfish thief"; the title of king hangs "loose about him, like a giant's robe" (V, ii, 26–28). . . .

The authority of the chief of Scottish magistrates is represented in *Macbeth* by the garment or cloak of office. When the garment is worn by Duncan, it is a garment of virtue. For Macbeth, the garment functions as sheep's clothing to disguise his wolfish nature. As a symbol, however, the garment of rule ought to be associated with a further level of meaning. Protestant theologians in England had emphasized the symbolism of clothes in their sermons and treatises: God has clothed his elect "with the garments of salvation, and . . . with the robe of righteousness." (*Isaiah* lxi, 10). . . .

MACBETH'S HYPOCRISY LEADS TO DESPAIR

Hypocrisy is also the theme which finds illustration in *Macbeth* through the imagery of the stage, which is very closely linked with the clothes imagery. In Act V, the hypocritical Macbeth has come to the desperate conclusion that "Life's but a walking shadow; a poor player,/ That struts and frets his hour upon the stage,/ And then is heard no more" (V, v, 28–30). Life for him is emptied of all meaning, and the outward appearance has become for him all that there is. Thus Macbeth has destroyed all moral distinctions and indeed all values. For him, a counterfeit coin would seem to be worth as much as the "golden stamp" which Edward the Confessor[3] hangs about the necks of those whom he touches for the king's evil. The audience, however, should know enough not to believe Macbeth's words in V, v: the "tomorrow" speech is directly opposed to the orthodox views which we may believe Shakespeare accepted. Contemporary sermons make the commonplace connections which are necessary for a right understanding of the stage imagery. [In *Foure Sermons*] Thomas Carew says:

> An hypocrite, is as much to say, as a counterfeit or dissembler; the word is borrowed from stage players, who put on them the persons and apparel of other men, as some put on the robes, and play the part of kings; and so liers, being no such, but in counterfeit show.

3. king of England, 1042–1066

. . . The criminal and hypocrite, who plays the part of an innocent man, is nevertheless by his art not able to escape from morality and natural law. As George Downame notes [in his *Lectures*], "the hypocrite . . . by reason of his bad conscience is overtaken with fear. . . ." Fear certainly is a pervasive factor in Shakespeare's *Macbeth*, as [critic] Lily Campbell has shown so convincingly [in] *Shakespeare's Tragic Heroes*. Macbeth's conscience continues to condemn the malice within him until he has managed to kill conscience. Macbeth succeeds in throwing off the rulership of his conscience, and in the end his rebellion is in this sense complete. By V, v, when he hears the cry of the women at the death of his wife, Macbeth with appalling indifference can say:

> I have almost forgot the taste of fears:
> The time has been, my senses would have cooled
> To hear a night-shriek, and my fell of hair
> Would at a dismal Treatise rouse, and stir
> As life were in't.

> (V, v, 13–17)

Macbeth suffers from an infinite weariness of soul, yet this is also rant which discloses how hardened his soul now is. . . .

Ultimately, the path leads "to despair and death." Macbeth, having first falsely dressed himself in the robes and crown in his imagination, commits himself to the hopeless cause of crime which will lead him deeply into the wood of error. There he will find it to be "a forest of distrust and fear" through which he will pass to the deepest despair.

Macbeth does despair, since in I, vii he gives up all hope of "the life of the world to come." Led by the cunning of the evil sisters, he is cozened into trading heavenly hope for an earthly crown. When the murder of Duncan is discovered, he himself recognizes that had he "died an hour before this chance,/ I had lived a blessed time" (II, iii, 112–113). Macbeth's desperation is conventional: It is a sin through which he "dispaireth utterly, and is past all hope of the good will of God, verily thinking that his naughtiness, or sins, excel the mercies and goodness of God. . . ."[4] Like Judas and Faustus,[5] Macbeth believes that his crime is too great to be forgiven.

The despair which Macbeth feels is deepened when he realizes that the crown he wears is "fruitless" and the

4. according to Willymat's *Physicke, to Cure the Most Dangerous Disease of Desperation*
5. Judas betrayed Jesus; Faustus sold his soul to the devil.

scepter he carries is "barren." Seeing himself cut off from truth and life, Macbeth can neither receive nor can he pass life on. . . .

LADY MACBETH'S SELF-ACCUSATION AND DESPAIR

In III, ii, 8–11, Lady Macbeth reveals the despair which has come into her soul. During Acts I and II, she had brazenly urged her husband on to do destruction upon the life of Duncan. Now she realizes that

> Naught's had, all's spent,
> Where our desire is got without content:
> 'Tis safer, to be that which we destroy,
> Than by destruction dwell in doubtful joy.

To think of her condition in this way will shortly make her mad. Being on the side of destruction, she has helped to destroy the chains of God's love and mercy and goodness which bind the social and political order into its natural wholeness. So in her own mind she has given way to the worst kind of terrors, signs of disorder in the breast of one whose soul is out of harmony with the divine order. At night, she walks in her sleep and speaks "what she should not" (V, i, 49). . . .

Lady Macbeth does not repent. Her anguish stems from self-accusation which finds no outlet in penitence. Thus she suffers pangs which are like those experienced by the damned at the day of doom. In Sackville's "Induction," an allegorical "Remorse of conscience" sits inside the jaws of hell:

> So was her mind continually in fear,
> Tossed and tormented with the tedious thought
> Of those detested crimes which she had wrought.

She wishes "for death, and yet she could not die."[6] Lady Macbeth also must remember the horror of the night Duncan was killed—"who would have thought the old man to have had so much blood in him?" (V, i, 39–41). Her mind cannot forget the crimes which she and her husband have committed, but she is unable to ease the burden which rests upon her heart. . . .

MACBETH BECOMES A TYRANT

Macbeth's despair progresses in a different direction, though in the end he also, being weary of life, wishes for death. Macbeth's heart becomes hardened as did Pharaoh's and

---

6. Thomas Sackville (1536–1608) is a contributor to *Mirror for Magistrates*, an anthology recounting the downfall of illustrious English people.

Herod's.[7] Unlike his wife, who gains progressive understanding of her sin and thus is overcome by her despair,
Macbeth successfully does stop up the passages which lead
to remorse. He becomes a callous thug, a criminal who,
once he has crept into credit, proceeds to use the most ruthless methods of tyranny. Macbeth's apostacy[8] deprives him
of all sensitivity and intelligence; he is thus utterly "deprived
of heavenly light and life" (*Homilies*, p. 71). It is not that Fate
has entered the lists to fight against the protagonist. . . .

Macbeth is the story of the making of a tyrant, but typically Macbeth's raging and boasting in Act V is not so simple
as it might at first seem. Scenes of brashness and bragging
are alternated with scenes which show all the emptiness
and deadness of Macbeth's position. The famous "tomorrow" speech (V, v, 23–32) emphatically does not demonstrate anything like Shakespeare's own "philosophical inco-
herence," but it does point out that *for Macbeth himself*, all
coherence is gone. Time seems to him to creep on from day
to day without any sense of direction or purpose, while at
that very moment the hand of God is actually at work di-
recting his forces, which are assembled under Malcolm, so
that his will may be executed in history. Macbeth is the fool
who will be lighted to his death, which is symbolized by the
extinguishing of the "brief Candle." [Critic] R.M. Frye notes
that pastors of the English Church commonly compared human life to "a candlelight which is soon blown out." For the
protagonist of Act V, life is but "a tale/ Told by an idiot, full
of sound and fury/ Signifying nothing." This is indeed a terrifying vision of human existence. Macbeth has killed reason within himself. He can no longer apprehend the order of
the universe which impressed itself upon him in earlier
scenes. The "tomorrow" speech gives us life utterly without
hope. The full force of Macbeth's despair is brought home to
the audience. . . .

Transgressing the natural laws which any rightful king
would have held inviolate, the tyrant in Act V does not so
much reign as rage. His subjects do not voluntarily obey his
behests, but are moved only by fear of his power. He is isolated from humanity. No honor, love, or friendship is offered

---

7. The Pharaoh was a tyrant king of ancient Egypt; Herod was king of Judea, 40–4 B.C.,
who, according to the New Testament, tried to kill the child Jesus by having all children under age two in Bethlehem put to death.   8. abandonment of one's religious
faith, political party, or principles

to him, nor does he look to have them. Instead, his people curse him and reluctantly give him "mouth-honor" (V, iii, 31–33). The noble Macbeth's glory has all passed away. In Act V, he goes forth alone to the battlefield accompanied by his "slaughterous thoughts." The last act of butchery which we see on stage is the killing of young Siward. Of Macbeth's name, young Siward cries: "The devil himself could not pronounce a title/ More hateful to mine ear" (V, vii, 13–14).

Though in V, vii, 20 he can smile at swords and "Weapons laugh to scorn," Macbeth will shortly meet with sudden death at the hands of Macduff. His men desert to join the instruments of good; he apparently knows that the battle is lost. The struggle between vice and virtue has already been settled in favor of the latter. Yet in his pride Macbeth refuses to go the way of his wife, but instead means to extend further the destruction upon the forces of good. When first confronted with Macduff, however, he falters, though he still believes that his antagonist will not be able to make him bleed. Macbeth shortly discovers that Macduff represents the flood of God's destruction which will overcome the life of the hardened tyrant.

To Macbeth, the day of doom has come. It is indeed a dismal day for him when his hollow world collapses. He has been "a-weary of the sun," even wishing that "the estate of the world were now undone" (V, v, 56–57). Utter "wrack" does come to him, and he is ignominiously beheaded by the Thane of Fife whom he had wronged. True, he has a chance to live for a while yet, but in his weariness he has no wish to be exhibited "as our rarer monsters are" in the triumph which shall follow Malcolm's victory. He "will not yield" (V, viii, 34) but must meet his end this day. It is the final act of tragic self-annihilation which stems from his early tragic yielding to demonic temptation. In the final analysis, Macbeth must be judged guilty of great folly. He is representative of the tragic waste which evil is able to achieve "in this earthly world."

Poetry of Evil

L.C. Knights

L.C. Knights argues that *Macbeth* is poetry expressing evil in three interwoven themes: the reversal of
values, reversal of the natural order, and confusion
resulting from deceitful appearances. Knight's analysis shows that all three themes emerge in the first
act and are developed in the next two, and that images of religion and the natural order are significant
in clarifying the theme of evil. Act 5 recapitulates the
themes. L.C. Knights taught English at Cambridge
University in England. He is the author of *Shakespeare's Politics, Shakespeare: The Histories, An Approach to Hamlet,* and *Some Shakespearean Themes.*

Macbeth is a statement of evil. . . . It also happens to be poetry, which means that the apprehension of the whole can
only be obtained from a lively attention to the parts, whether
they have an immediate bearing on the main action or "illustrate character," or not. Two main themes, which can
only be separated for the purpose of analysis, are blended in
the play—the themes of the reversal of values and of unnatural disorder. And closely related to each is a third theme,
that of the deceitful appearance, and consequent doubt, uncertainty and confusion. . . .

Each theme is stated in the first act. The first scene, every
word of which will bear the closest scrutiny, strikes one
dominant chord:

> Faire is foule, and foule is faire,
> Hover through the fogge and filthie ayre.

It is worth remarking that "Hurley-burley" implies more
than "the tumult of sedition or insurrection." Both it and
"when the Battaile's lost, and wonne" suggest the kind of
metaphysical pitch-and-toss that is about to be played with
good and evil. At the same time we hear the undertone of
uncertainty: the scene opens with a question, and the second

Reprinted from L.C. Knights, "How Many Children Had Lady Macbeth?" in *Explorations: Essays In Criticism Mainly on the Literature of the Seventeenth Century* (New
York: New York University Press, 1964).

line suggests a region where the elements are disintegrated as they never are in nature; thunder and lightning are disjoined, and offered as alternatives. We should notice also that the scene expresses the same movement as the play as a whole: the general crystallizes into the immediate particular ("Where the place?"—"Upon the Heath."—"There to meet with Macbeth.") and then dissolves again into the general presentment of hideous gloom. All is done with the greatest speed, economy, and precision.

The second scene is full of images of confusion. . . . The description

> —Doubtfull it stood,
> As two spent Swimmers, that doe cling together,
> And choake their Art—[1]

applies not only to the battle but to the ambiguity of Macbeth's future fortunes. The impression conveyed is not only one of violence but of unnatural violence. . . .

In Act I, scene iii, confusion is succeeded by uncertainty. The Witches

> looke not like th' Inhabitants o' th' Earth,
> And yet are on't.

When they vanish, "what seem'd corporall" melts "as breath into the Winde." The whole force of the uncertainty of the scene is gathered into Macbeth's soliloquy,

> This supernaturall solliciting[2]
> Cannot be ill; cannot be good . . .

which with its sickening see-saw rhythm completes the impression of "a phantasma, or a hideous dream." Macbeth's echoing of the Witches' "Faire is foule" has often been commented upon.

STATING THE NATURAL ORDER

In contrast to the preceding scenes, Act I, scene iv, suggests the natural order which is shortly to be violated. It stresses: natural relationships—"children," "servants," "sons," and "kinsmen"; honourable bonds and the political order—"liege," "thanes," "service," "duty," "loyalty," "throne," "state," and "honour"; and the human "love" is linked to the natural order of organic growth by images of husbandry. . . .

At this point something should be said of what is meant by "the natural order." In *Macbeth* this comprehends both

---

1. **choake . . . Art:** i.e., prevent each other from swimming 2. **solliciting:** incitement

"wild nature"—birds, beasts, and reptiles—and humankind since "humane statute purg'd the gentle Weale." The specifically human aspect is related to the concept of propriety and degree. . . . In short, it represents society in harmony with nature, bound by love and friendship, and ordered by law and duty. It is one of the main axes of reference by which we take our emotional bearings in the play.

In the light of this the scene of Duncan's entry into the castle gains in significance. The critics have often remarked on the irony. What is not so frequently observed is that the key words of the scene are "loved," "wooingly," "bed," "procreant Cradle," "breed, and haunt," all images of love and procreation, supernaturally sanctioned, for the associations of "temple-haunting" colour the whole of the speeches of Banquo and Duncan. . . .

MURDER PRESENTED AS UNNATURAL

The murder is explicitly presented as unnatural. After the greeting of Ross and Angus, Macbeth's heart knocks at his ribs "against the use of Nature." Lady Macbeth fears his "humane kindnesse"; she wishes herself "unsexed," that she may be troubled by "no compunctious visitings of Nature," and invokes the "murth'ring Ministers" who "wait on Natures Mischiefe." The murder is committed when

> Nature seemes dead, and wicked Dreames abuse
> The Curtain'd³ sleepe,

and it is accompanied by portents "unnaturall, even like the deed that's done." The sun remains obscured, and Duncan's horses "Turn'd wilde in nature." Besides these explicit references to the unnatural we notice the violence of the imagery—

> I have given Sucke, and know
> How tender 'tis to love the Babe that milkes me,
> I would, while it was smyling in my Face,
> Have pluckt my Nipple from his Bonelesse Gummes,
> And dasht the Braines out.

Not only are the feelings presented unnatural in this sense, they are also strange—peculiar compounds which cannot be classified by any of the usual labels—"fear," "disgust," etc. Macbeth's words towards the end of Act II, scene i, serve to illustrate this:

> Thou sowre [sure] and firme-set Earth
> Heare not my steps, which way they walke, for feare

3. **curtain'd:** with bed curtains drawn

> Thy very stones prate of my where-about,
> And take the present horror[4] from the time,
> Which now sutes with it.

The first three lines imply a recognition of the enormity of the crime; Macbeth asks that the earth ("sure and firme-set" contrasted with the disembodied "Murder" which "moves like a Ghost") shall not hear his steps, for if it does so the very stones will speak and betray him—thereby breaking the silence and so lessening the horror. . . .

"Confusion now hath made his Master-peece," and in the lull that follows the discovery of the murder, Ross and an Old Man, as chorus, echo the theme of unnatural disorder. . . . And an overtone of meaning takes our thoughts to Macbeth, whose attempt to make good of bad by restoring the natural order is the theme of the next movement; the tragedy lies in his inevitable failure. . . .

THE CONFUSION OF THE FEAST AND THE BANQUET SCENE

At the beginning of the scene, we remember, Macbeth had arranged "a feast," "a solemn supper," at which "society" should be "welcome." And when alone he suggests the ancient harmonies by rejecting in idea the symbols of their contraries—"a fruitlesse Crowne," "a barren Scepter," and an "unlineall" succession. But this new "health" is "sickly" whilst Banquo lives, and can only be made "perfect" by his death. In an attempt to re-create an order based on murder, disorder makes fresh inroads. This is made explicit in the next scene (III.ii). Here the snake, usually represented as the most venomous of creatures, stands for the natural order which Macbeth has "scotched" but which will "close, and be her selfe."

At this point in the play there is a characteristic confusion. At the end of Act III, scene ii, Macbeth says, "Things bad begun, make strong themselves by ill," that is, all that he can do is to ensure his physical security by a second crime, although earlier (III.i.106–107) he had aimed at complete "health" by the death of Banquo and Fleance, and later he says that the murder of Fleance would have made him

> perfect,
> Whole as the Marble, founded as the Rocke.

(III.iv.21–22)

---

4. **present horror:** i.e., the silence of midnight

The truth is only gradually disentangled from this illusion.

The situation is magnificently presented in the banquet scene. Here speech, action, and symbolism combine. The stage direction "*Banquet prepar'd*" is the first pointer. In Shakespeare, as Mr. Wilson Knight has remarked, banquets are almost invariably symbols of rejoicing, friendship, and concord. Significantly, the nobles sit in due order.

> *Macbeth.*   You know your owne degrees,[5] sit downe:
> At first and last, the hearty welcome.

. . . There is no need for comment. In a sense the scene marks the climax of the play. One avenue has been explored; "Society," "Host," "Hostess," "Friends" and "Welcome" repeat a theme which henceforward is heard only faintly until it is taken up in the final orchestration, when it appears as "Honor, Love, Obedience, Troopes of Friends." With the disappearance of the ghost, Macbeth may be "a man againe," but he has, irretrievably,

> displac'd[6] the mirth,
> Broke the good meeting, wich most admir'd[7] disorder.

The end of the scene is in direct contrast to its beginning.

> Stand not upon the order of your going,
> But go at once

echoes ironically, "You know your owne degrees, sit downe.". . .

THE PLAY MOVES FORWARD INDIRECTLY

Although the play moves swiftly, it does not move with a simple directness. Its complex subtleties include crosscurrents, the ebb and flow of opposed thoughts and emotions. The scene in Macduff's castle, made up of doubts, riddles, paradoxes, and uncertainties, ends with an affirmation, "Thou ly'st thou shaggeear'd Villaine." But this is immediately followed, not by the downfall of Macbeth, but by a long scene which takes up once more the theme of mistrust, disorder and evil. . . .

Obviously Macduff's audience with Malcolm and the final determination to invade Scotland help on the story, but this is of subordinate importance. It is clear also that Malcolm's suspicion and the long testing of Macduff emphasize the mistrust that has spread from the central evil of the play. . . .

---

5. **degrees:** ranks. This is a state banquet at which each guest sits according to his rank. 6. **displac'd:** upset 7. **admir'd:** to be wondered at

> Not in the Legions
> Of horrid Hell, can come a Divell more damn'd
> In evils, to top *Macbeth.*

> I grant him Bloody,
> Luxurious,[8] Avaricious, False, Deceitfull,
> Sodaine, Malicious, smacking of every sinne
> That has a name.

. . . His lines repeat and magnify the evils that have already been attributed to Macbeth, acting as a mirror wherein the ills of Scotland are reflected. And the statement of evil is strengthened by contrast with the opposite virtues, "As justice, Verity, Temperance, Stablenesse.". . .

I have called *Macbeth* a statement of evil; but it is a statement not of a philosophy but of ordered emotion. This ordering is of course a continuous process (hence the importance of the scrupulous analysis of each line), it is not merely something that happens in the last act corresponding to the dénouement or unravelling of the plot. All the same the interests aroused are heightened in the last act before they are finally "placed," and we are given a vantage point from which the whole course of the drama may be surveyed in retrospect. . . .

THE ASSOCIATION OF GOOD WITH RELIGIOUS SYMBOLS

At this point it is necessary to return to what I have already said about the importance of images of grace and of the holy supernatural in the play. For the last hundred years or so the critics have not only sentimentalized Macbeth—ignoring the completeness with which Shakespeare shows his final identification with evil—but they have slurred the passages in which the positive good is presented by means of religious symbols. . . . Macduff has fled to "the pious Edward," "the Holy King," who has received Malcolm "with such grace." Lennox prays for the aid of "some holy Angell,"

> that a swift blessing
> May soone returne to this our suffering Country,
> Under a hand accurs'd.

And the "other Lord" answers, "He send my Prayers with him." Many of the phrases are general and abstract—"grace," "the malevolence of Fortune," "his high respect"—but one passage has an individual particularity that gives it prominence:

8. **luxurious:** lustful

> That by the helpe of these (with him above
> To ratifie the Worke) we may againe
> Give to our Tables meate, sleepe to our Nights:
> Free from our Feasts, and Banquets bloody knives;
> Do faithful Homage, and receive free Honors,[9]
> All which we pine for now.

Food and sleep, society and the political order are here, as before, represented as supernaturally sanctioned. . . .

Scattered notes ("Gracious England," "Christendome," "heaven," "gentle Heavens") remind us of the theme until the end of the scene, when we know that Macbeth (the "Hell-Kite," "this Fiend of Scotland")

> Is ripe for shaking, and the Power above
> Put on their Instruments.

The words quoted are not mere formalities; they have a positive function, and help to determine the way in which we shall respond to the final scenes.

DISEASE, DISORDER AND THE UNNATURAL IN ACT V

The description of the King's Evil (IV.iii.141–159) has a particular relevance; it is directly connected with the disease metaphors of the last Act; and these are strengthened by combining within themselves the ideas of disorder and of the unnatural which run throughout the play. . . .

The images of health and disease are clearly related to moral good and evil. The Doctor says of Lady Macbeth,

> More needs she the Divine, than the Physitian:
> God, God forgive us all.

Macbeth asks him,

> Can'st thou not Minister to a minde diseas'd,
> Plucke from the Memory a rooted Sorrow,
> Raze out the written troubles of the Braine,
> And with some sweet Oblivious Antidote
> Cleanse the stufft[10] bosome, of that perillous stuffe
> Which weighes upon the heart?

There is terrible irony in his reply to the Doctor's "Therein the Patient must minister to himselfe": "Throw Physicke to the Dogs, He none of it." We have already noticed the association of the ideas of disease and of the unnatural in these final scenes—

> unnatural deeds
> Do breed unnatural troubles,

---

9. **free honors:** honors bestowed on freemen, and not as a reward for a crime. 10. **stufft:** overfull

. . . But the unnatural has now another part to play, in the peculiar "reversal" that takes place at the end of *Macbeth.* Hitherto the agent of the unnatural has been Macbeth. Now it is Malcolm who commands Birnam Wood to move, it is "the good Macduff" who reveals his unnatural birth, and the opponents of Macbeth whose "deere causes" would "excite the mortified man." Hitherto Macbeth has been the deceiver, "mocking the time with fairest show"; now Malcolm orders,

> Let every Souldier hew him downe a Bough,
> And bear't before him, thereby shall we shadow[11]
> The numbers of our Hoast, and make discovery
> Erre in report of us.

By associating with the opponents of evil the ideas of deceit and of the unnatural, previously associated solely with Macbeth and the embodiments of evil, Shakespeare emphasizes the disorder and at the same time frees our minds from the burden of the horror. After all, the movement of Birnam Wood and Macduff's unnatural birth have a simple enough explanation. . . .

If we merely read the play we are liable to overlook the importance of the sights and sounds which are obvious on the stage. The frequent stage directions should be observed— *Drum and Colours, Enter Malcolm . . . and Soldiers Marching, A Cry within of Women*—and there are continuous directions for *Alarums, Flourishes,* and fighting. Macduff orders,

> Make all our Trumpets speak, give them all breath,
> Those clamorous Harbingers of Blood, and Death,

and he traces Macbeth by the noise of fighting. . . .

But all this disorder has now a positive tendency, towards the good which Macbeth had attempted to destroy, and which he names as "Honor, Love, Obedience, Troopes of Friends." At the beginning of the battle Malcolm says,

> Cosins, I hope the dayes are neere at hand
> That Chambers will be safe.[12] . . .

By now there should be no danger of our misinterpreting the greatest of Macbeth's final speeches.

> To morrow, and to morrow, and to morrow,
> Creepes in this petty pace from day to day,
> To the last syllable of Recorded time.
> And all our yesterdays, have lighted Fooles
> The way to dusty death. Out, out, breefe Candle.

---

11. **shadow:** conceal 12. **Chambers . . . safe:** i.e., a man will have nothing to fear in his own house

Life's but a walking Shadow, a poore Player,
That struts and frets his houre upon the Stage,
And then is heard no more. It is a Tale
Told by an Ideot, full of sound and fury
Signifying nothing.

The theme of the false appearance is revived—with a difference. It is not only that Macbeth sees life as deceitful, but the
poetry is so fine that we are almost bullied into accepting an
essential ambiguity in the final statement of the play, as
though Shakespeare were expressing his own "philosophy"
in the lines. But the lines are "placed" by the tendency of the
last Act (order emerging from disorder, truth emerging from
behind deceit), culminating in the recognition of the
Witches' equivocation ("And be these Jugling Fiends no
more believ'd . . ."), the death of Macbeth, and the last words
of Siward, Macduff, and Malcolm (V.vii.64–105).

This tendency has behind it the whole weight of the positive values which Shakespeare has already established, and
which are evoked in Macbeth's speech—

My way of life
Is falne into the Sear,[13] the yellow Leafe,
And that which should accompany Old-Age,
As Honor, Love, Obedience, Troopes of Friends,
I must not looke to have: but in their stead,
Curses, not lowd but deepe, Mouth-honor, breath
Which the poore heart would faine deny, and dare not.

13. **sear:** dry and withered

Shakespeare's Imagery Heightens Emotions

Caroline F.E. Spurgeon

Caroline F.E. Spurgeon's analysis of *Macbeth* illustrates the abundance and subtlety of Shakespeare's imagery. Caroline F.E. Spurgeon was professor emerita of English literature at the University of London. She is the author of *Shakespeare's Iterative Imagery*, a reprint of the 1931 annual Shakespeare lecture of the British Academy, and *Keats's Shakespeare*.

The imagery in *Macbeth* appears to me to be more rich and varied, more highly imaginative, more unapproachable by any other writer, than that of any other single play. It is particularly so, I think, in the continuous use made of the simplest, humblest, everyday things, drawn from the daily life in a small house, as a vehicle for sublime poetry. But that is beside our point here.

The ideas in the imagery are in themselves more imaginative, more subtle and complex than in other plays, and there are a greater number of them, interwoven the one with the other, recurring and repeating. There are at least four of these main ideas, and many subsidiary ones.

One is the picture of Macbeth himself.

MACBETH IN ILL-FITTING CLOTHES

Few simple things—harmless in themselves—have such a curiously humiliating and degrading effect as the spectacle of a notably small man enveloped in a coat far too big for him. Comic actors know this well—Charlie Chaplin, for instance—and it is by means of this homely picture that Shakespeare shows us his imaginative view of the hero, and expresses the fact that the honours for which the murders were committed are, after all, of very little worth to him.

The idea constantly recurs that Macbeth's new honours

sit ill upon him, like a loose and badly fitting garment, belonging to someone else. Macbeth himself first expresses it, quite early in the play, when, immediately following the first appearance of the witches and their prophecies, Ross arrives from the king, and greets him as thane of Cawdor, to which Macbeth quickly replies,

> The thane of Cawdor lives: why do you dress me
> In borrow'd robes?

(I.iii.108)

And a few minutes later, when he is rapt in ambitious thoughts suggested by the confirmation of two out of the three 'prophetic greetings', Banquo, watching him, murmurs,

> New honours come upon him,
> Like our strange garments, cleave not to their mould
> But with the aid of use.

(I.iii.144)

When Duncan is safely in the castle, Macbeth's better nature for a moment asserts itself, and, in debate with himself, he revolts from the contemplated deed for a threefold reason: because of its incalculable results, the treachery of such action from one who is both kinsman and host, and Duncan's own virtues and greatness as king.

When his wife joins him, his repugnance to the deed is as great, but it is significant that he gives three quite different reasons for not going ahead with it, reasons which he hopes may appeal to her, for he knows the others would not. So he urges that he has been lately honoured by the king, people think well of him, and therefore he should reap the reward of these things at once, and not upset everything by this murder which they have planned.

There is irony in the fact that to express the position he uses the same metaphor of clothes:

> I have bought
> Golden opinions from all sorts of people,
> Which would be worn now in their newest gloss,
> Not cast aside so soon.

(I.vii.32)

To which Lady Macbeth, quite unmoved, retorts contemptuously:

> Was the hope drunk
> Wherein you dress'd yourself?

(I.vii.36)

After the murder, when Ross says he is going to Scone for Macbeth's coronation, Macduff uses the same simile:

> Well, may you see things well done there: adieu!
> Lest our old robes sit easier than our new!
>
> (II.iv.37)

And, at the end, when the tyrant is at bay at Dunsinane, and the English troops are advancing, the Scottish lords still have this image in their minds. Caithness sees him as a man vainly trying to fasten a large garment on him with too small a belt:

> He cannot buckle his distemper'd cause
> Within the belt of rule;
>
> (V.ii.15)

while Angus, in a similar image, vividly sums up the essence of what they all have been thinking ever since Macbeth's accession to power:

> now does he feel his title
> Hang loose about him, like a giant's robe
> Upon a dwarfish thief.
>
> (V.ii.20)

This imaginative picture of a small, ignoble man encumbered and degraded by garments unsuited to him, should be put against the view emphasised by some critics (notably Coleridge and Bradley[1]) of the likeness between Macbeth and Milton's Satan in grandeur and sublimity.

Undoubtedly Macbeth is built on great lines and in heroic proportions, with great possibilities—there could be no tragedy else. He is great, magnificently great, in courage, in passionate, indomitable ambition, in imagination and capacity to feel. But he could never be put beside, say Hamlet or Othello, in nobility of nature; and there *is* an aspect in which he is but a poor, vain, cruel, treacherous creature, snatching ruthlessly over the dead bodies of kinsman and friend at place and power he is utterly unfitted to possess. It is worth remembering that it is thus that Shakespeare, with his unshrinking clarity of vision, repeatedly *sees* him.

SOUND ECHOING OVER VAST SPACE

Another image or idea which runs through *Macbeth* is the reverberation of sound echoing over vast regions, even into the limitless spaces beyond the confines of the world. Echo-

---

1. Samuel Taylor Coleridge, British Romantic poet, wrote *Shakespearean Criticism*; A.C. Bradley wrote *Shakespearean Tragedy*.

ing sound, as also reflected light, always interested Shake-speare; he is very quick to notice it, and in the earlier plays he records it often, quite simply and directly, as in the re-verberating roll of drums in *King John,* the smack of Petru-chio's kiss resounding through the church, Juliet's delicate picture of Echo with her airy tongue repeating 'Romeo', Vi-ola's assertion that were she Orsino, she would make the

> babbling gossip of the air
> Cry out 'Olivia!'
>
> (*Twelfth Night* I.v.283)

or her more fanciful remark to the duke that the tune he likes

> gives a very echo to the seat
> Where love is throned.
>
> (*TN* II.iv.21)

He specially loves, and describes repeatedly (in A *Midsum-mer Night's Dream, Titus Andronicus* and *The Taming of the Shrew*), the re-echoing sound of hounds and horn,

> the musical confusion
> Of hounds and echo in conjunction;
>
> (*MND* IV.i.115)

its doubling and mocking quality attracts him:

> the babbling echo mocks the hounds,
> Replying shrilly to the well-tuned horns,
> As if a double hunt were heard at once;
>
> (*TA* II.ii.117)

and it is this quality which Warwick applies most appositely when, having been roused in the small hours to soothe the sleepless and fretful king, he finally loses patience with Henry's fears that the revolutionaries must be fifty thousand strong, and retorts, somewhat tartly,

> It cannot be, my lord;
> Rumour doth double, like the voice and echo,
> The numbers of the fear'd. Please it your grace
> To go to bed.
>
> (*2 Henry IV* III.i.96)

It is not until after 1600, and most noticeably in *Troilus and Cressida,* that Shakespeare uses this same idea of rever-beration and reflection to illustrate subtle and philosophic thought. Ulysses' mind is full of it, and he applies it con-stantly; Kent, in *King Lear,* seizes on an analogous natural fact to point the truth that noise and protestation do not nec-essarily indicate deep feeling; while in *Macbeth,* the peculiar

quality of echoing and re-echoing sound is used to emphasise, in the most highly imaginative and impressive way, a
thought constantly present with Shakespeare in his middle
years, the incalculable and boundless effects of evil in the
nature of one man.

Macbeth himself, like Hamlet, is fully conscious of how
impossible it is to 'trammel up the consequence' (I.vii.3) of
his deed, and by his magnificent images of angels pleading
trumpet-tongued,

> And pity, like a naked, new-born babe,
> Striding the blast, or heaven's cherubin horsed
> Upon the sightless couriers of the air,

> (I.vii.21)

who

> Shall blow the horrid deed in every eye,
> That tears shall drown the wind,

> (I.vii.24)

he fills our imagination with the picture of its being broad-
cast through great spaces with reverberating sound.

This is taken up again by Macduff, when he cries,

> each new morn
> New widows howl, new orphans cry, new sorrows
> Strike heaven on the face, that it resounds
> As if it felt with Scotland and yell'd out
> Like syllable of dolour[2];

> (IV.iii.4)

and again by Ross, when he is trying to break the terrible
news of Macbeth's latest murders to Macduff—the destruction of his own wife and children—

> I have words
> That would be howl'd out in the desert air,
> Where hearing should not latch them.

> (IV.iii.193)

One can scarcely conceive a more vivid picture of the vastnesses
of space than this, and of the overwhelming and unending nature of the consequences or reverberations of the evil deed.

LIGHT SYMBOLIZES LIFE AND GOODNESS; DARKNESS SYMBOLIZES EVIL AND DEATH

Another constant idea in the play arises out of the symbolism that light stands for life, virtue, goodness; and darkness

---

2. **that . . . dolour:** Even the heavens resound as if they echoed the lamentations of
Scotland.

for evil and death. 'Angels are bright', (IV.iii.22) the witches are 'secret, black and midnight hags', (IV.i.48) and, as [critic Edward] Dowden says, the movement of the whole play might be summed up in the words, 'good things of day begin to droop and drowse'. (III.ii.52)

This is, of course, very obvious, but out of it develops the further thought which is assumed throughout, that the evil which is being done is so horrible that it would blast the sight to look on it; so that darkness, or partial blinding, is necessary to carry it out.

Like so much in the play it is ironic that it should be Duncan who first starts this simile, the idea of which turns into a leading motive in the tragedy. When he is conferring the new honour on his son, he is careful to say that others, kinsmen and thanes, will also be rewarded:

> signs of nobleness, like stars, shall shine
> On all deservers.
>
> (I.iv.41)

No sooner has the king spoken, than Macbeth realises that Malcolm, now a prince of the realm, is an added obstacle in his path, and suddenly, shrinking from the blazing horror of the murderous thought which follows, he cries to himself,

> Stars, hide your fires;
> Let not light see my black and deep desires.
>
> (I.iv.50)

From now on, the idea that only in darkness can such evil deeds be done is ever present with both Macbeth and his wife, as is seen in their two different and most characteristic invocations to darkness: her blood-curdling cry,

> Come, thick night,
> And pall thee in the dunnest smoke of hell,
>
> (I.v.51)

which takes added force when we hear later the poignant words, 'She has light by her continually' (V.i.23); and his more gentle appeal in the language of falconry,

> Come, seeling night,
> Scarf up the tender eye of pitiful day.
>
> (III.ii.46)

And when Banquo, sleepless, uneasy, with heart heavy as lead, crosses the courtyard on the fateful night, with Fleance holding the flaring torch before him, and, looking up to the dark sky, mutters,

> There's husbandry in heaven,
> Their candles are all out,
>
> (II.i.4)

we know the scene is set for treachery and murder. So it is fitting that on the day following, 'dark night strangles the travelling lamp', and

> darkness does the face of earth entomb,
> When living light should kiss it.
>
> (II.iv.9)

The idea of deeds which are too terrible for human eyes to look on is also constant; Lady Macbeth scoffs it—'the sleeping and the dead', she argues, 'are but as pictures':

> 'tis the eye of childhood
> That fears a painted devil;
>
> (II.ii.53–55)

but Macduff, having seen the slain king, rushes out, and cries to Lennox,

> Approach the chamber, and destroy your sight
> With a new Gorgon.[3]
>
> (II.iii.76)

Macbeth boldly asserts he dare look on that 'which might appal the devil' (III.iv.60), and the bitterness of defeat he realises on seeing one 'too like the spirit of Banquo' in the procession of kings, is expressed in his agonised cry,

> Thy crown does sear mine eye-balls;
>
> (IV.i.113)

while in his bitter and beautiful words at the close, the dominant thoughts and images are the quenching of light and the empty reverberation of sound and fury, 'signifying nothing'. (V.v.28)

SIN CAST AS DISEASE

The fourth of the chief symbolic ideas in the play is one which is very constant with Shakespeare, and is to be found all through his work, that sin is a disease—Scotland is sick.

So Macbeth, while repudiating physic for himself, turns to the doctor and says if he could, by analysis, find Scotland's disease

> And purge it to a sound and pristine health,
> I would applaud thee to the very echo,
> That should applaud again . . .

---

3. in Greek mythology any of the three sisters—Stheno, Euryale, and Medusa—who had snakes for hair, and eyes that turned anyone looking into them into stone

What rhubarb, senna, or what purgative drug,
Would scour these English hence?

(V.iii.52–56)

Malcolm speaks of his country as weeping, bleeding and wounded, and later urges Macduff to

make us medicines of our great revenge,
To cure this deadly grief;

(IV.iii.214)

while Caithness calls Malcolm himself the 'medicine of the sickly weal', 'the country's purge'. (V.ii.27)

It is worth noting that all Macbeth's images of sickness are remedial or soothing in character: balm for a sore, sleep after fever, a purge, physic for pain, a 'sweet oblivious antidote' (V.iii.43); thus intensifying to the reader or audience his passionate and constant longing for well-being, rest, and, above all, peace of mind.

IMAGES OF UNNATURALNESS, MOTION, BLOOD, AND ANIMALS

Other subsidiary motives in the imagery, which work in and out through the play, insensibly but deeply affect the reader's imagination. One of these is the idea of the *unnaturalness* of Macbeth's crime, that it is a convulsion of nature. This is brought out repeatedly and emphasised by imagery, as are also the terrible results of going against nature.

Macbeth himself says that Duncan's wounds

look'd like a breach in nature
For ruin's wasteful entrance,

(II.iii.118)

and Macduff speaks of his murder as the sacrilege of breaking open the Lord's anointed temple. The events which accompany and follow it are terrible because unnatural; an owl kills a falcon, horses eat each other, the earth was feverous and did shake, day becomes night; all this, says the old man, is unnatural,

Even like the deed that's done.

(II.iv.10)

Macbeth's greatest trouble is the unnatural one that he has murdered sleep, and the whole feeling of dislocation is increased by such images as 'let the frame of things disjoint' (III.ii.16), or by Macbeth's conjuration to the witches with the terrible list of the convulsions of nature which may result from their answering him. Indeed, if from one angle the movement of the play may be summed up in Macbeth's words,

> Good things of day begin to droop and drowse,
>
> (III.ii.52)

from another it is completely described by the doctor in his diagnosis of the doomed queen's malady as 'a great perturbation in nature'. (V.i.10)

In addition to these running images symbolising or expressing an idea, there are groups of others which might be called atmospheric in their effect, that is, they raise or increase certain feelings and emotions.

Such is the action of rapid riding, which contributes and emphasises a certain sense of rushing, relentless and goaded motion, of which we are very conscious in the play. This is symbolised externally by the rapid ride of the messenger to Lady Macbeth, arriving 'almost dead for breath' (I.v.37), ahead of Macbeth, who himself has outridden Duncan. The king remarks in unconscious irony,

> he rides well,
> And his great love, sharp as his spur, hath holp him
> To his home before us.
>
> (I.vi.22)

It is noticeable what a large part riding plays in the images which crowd on Macbeth's heated brain when he is weighing the *pros* and *cons* of his plan: the new-born babe 'striding the blast' (I.vii.22), heaven's cherubin horsed

> Upon the sightless couriers of the air,
>
> (I.vii.23)

and finally, the vision of his 'intent', his aim, as a horse lacking sufficient spur to action, which melts into the picture of his ambition as a rider vaulting into the saddle with such energy that it 'o'erleaps itself', and falls on the further side.

The feeling of fear, horror and pain is increased by the constant and recurring images of blood; these are very marked, and have been noticed by others, especially by Bradley, the most terrible being Macbeth's description of himself wading in a river of blood, while the most stirring to the imagination, perhaps in the whole of Shakespeare, is the picture of him gazing, rigid with horror, at his own blood-stained hand and watching it dye the whole green ocean red.

The images of animals also, nearly all predatory, unpleasant or fierce, add to this same feeling; such are a nest of scorpions, a venomous serpent and a snake, a 'hell-kite'[4] eating chickens, a devouring vulture, a swarm of insects, a tiger, rhinoceros and bear, the tiny wren fighting the owl for the life of her young, small birds with the fear of the net, lime, pitfall or gin, used with such bitter ironic effect by Lady Macduff and her boy just before they are murdered, the shrieking owl, and the bear tied to a stake fighting savagely to the end.

Enough has been said, I think, to indicate how complex and varied is the symbolism in the imagery of *Macbeth*, and to make it clear that an appreciable part of the emotions we feel throughout of pity, fear, and horror, is due to the subtle but definite and repeated action of this imagery upon our minds, of which, in our preoccupation with the main theme, we remain often largely unconscious.

4. a kite is a predatory bird

CHAPTER 4

Themes and Structure in *Macbeth*

READINGS ON
MACBETH

The Universe and Time in *Macbeth*

Mark Van Doren

Mark Van Doren calls *Macbeth*'s universe externally
and internally distorted, without a normal sense of
time. Van Doren describes a strange, dark, shifting
world of excess. Time, he maintains, finally loses
meaning. Mark Van Doren taught English at Columbia University. He is the author of *Collected Poems*, a
book of short stories, and the critical works *Henry
David Thoreau: A Critical Study, The Poetry of John
Dryden, Edwin Arlington Robinson, Studies in Metaphysical Poetry*, and *Hawthorne*.

"Macbeth" like "Lear" is all end; the difference appearing in
the speed with which doom rushes down, so that this rapidest
of tragedies suggests whirlwinds rather than glaciers, and in
the fact that terror rather than pity is the mode of the accom-
panying music. "Macbeth," then, is not in the fullest known
sense a tragedy. But we do not need to suppose that this is because important parts of it have been lost. More of it would
have had to be more of the same. And the truth is that no significant scene seems to be missing. "Macbeth" is incompara-
bly brilliant as it stands, and within its limits perfect. What it
does it does with flawless force. It hurls a universe against a
man, and if the universe that strikes is more impressive than
the man who is stricken, great as his size and gaunt as his
soul may be, there is no good reason for doubting that this is
what Shakespeare intended. The triumph of "Macbeth" is the
construction of a world, and nothing like it has ever been
constructed in twenty-one hundred lines.

A STRANGE AND DARK WORLD

This world, which is at once without and within Macbeth, can
be most easily described as "strange." The word, like the

witches, is always somewhere doing its work. Even in the battle which precedes the play the thane of Glamis has made "strange images of death" (I.ii.97), and when he comes home to his lady his face is "as a book where men may read strange matters" (I.v.63–4). Duncan's horses after his murder turn wild in nature and devour each other—"a thing most strange and certain" (II.iv.14). Nothing is as it should be in such a world. "Who would have thought the old man to have had so much blood in him?" (V.i.44–45). There is a drift of disorder in all events, and the air is murky with unwelcome miracles.

It is a dark world too, inhabited from the beginning by witches who meet on a blasted heath in thunder and lightning, and who hover through fog and filthy air as they leave on unspeakable errands. It is a world wherein "men must not walk too late" (III.vi.7), for the night that was so pretty in "Romeo and Juliet," "A Midsummer Night's Dream," and "The Merchant of Venice" has grown terrible with ill-smelling mists and the stench of blood. The time that was once a playground for free and loving spirits has closed like a trap, or yawned like a bottomless pit. The "dark hour" that Banquo borrows from the night is his last hour on an earth which has lost the distinction between sun and gloom.

> Darkness does the face of earth entomb,
> When living light should kiss it.
>
> (II.iv.9–10)

The second of these lines makes a sound that is notable in the play for its rarity: the sound of life in its normal ease and lightness. Darkness prevails because the witches, whom Banquo calls its instruments, have willed to produce it. But Macbeth is its instrument too, as well as its victim. And the Weïrd Sisters no less than he are expressions of an evil that employs them both and has roots running farther into darkness than the mind can guess.

A Shifting, Changing World

It is furthermore a world in which nothing is certain to keep its shape. Forms shift and consistencies alter, so that what was solid may flow and what was fluid may congeal to stone.

> The earth hath bubbles, as the water has,
> And these are of them,
>
> (I.iii. 79–80)

says Banquo of the vanished witches. Macbeth addresses the "sure and firm set earth" (II.i.56), but nothing could be less firm than the whole marble and the founded rock he has fancied his life to be. At the very moment he speaks he has seen a dagger which is not there, and the "strange infirmity" he confesses at the banquet will consist of seeing things that cannot be. His first apostrophe to the witches had been to creatures

That look not like the inhabitants o' the earth,
And yet are on 't.

(I.iii.41–42)

So now a dead man lives; Banquo's brains are out but he rises again, and "this is more strange than such a murder is."

Take any shape but that, and my firm nerves
Shall never tremble.

(III.iv.102–103)

But the shape of everything is wrong, and the nerves of Macbeth are never proof against trembling. The cardinal instance of transformation is himself. Bellona's[1] bridegroom has been turned to jelly.

The current of change pouring forever through this universe has, as a last effect, dissolved it. And the dissolution of so much that was solid has liberated deadly fumes, has thickened the air until it suffocates all breathers. If the footing under men is less substantial than it was, the atmosphere they must push through is almost too heavy for life. It is confining, swarming, swelling; it is viscous, it is sticky; and it threatens strangulation. All of the speakers in the play conspire to create the impression that this is so. Not only do the witches in their opening scene wail "Fair is foul, and foul is fair," but the military men who enter after them anticipate in their talk of recent battle the imagery of entanglement to come.

Doubtful it stood,
As two spent swimmers that do cling together
And choke their art. . . .
The multiplying villainies of nature
Do swarm upon him. . . .
So from that spring whence comfort seem'd to come
Discomfort swells.

(I.ii.7–28)

Macbeth's sword is reported to have "smok'd with bloody execution," and he and Banquo were "as cannons overcharg'd with double cracks;" they

Doubly redoubled strokes upon the foe.

1. in Roman mythology Bellona is the goddess of war

A WORLD OF EXCESS

The hyperbole is ominous, the excess is sinister. In the third scene, after what seemed corporal in the witches has melted into the wind, Ross and Angus join Banquo and Macbeth to report the praises of Macbeth that had poured in on Duncan "as thick as hail," and to salute the new thane of Cawdor. The witches then have been right in two respects, and Macbeth says in an aside:

> Two truths are told,
> As happy prologues to the swelling act
> Of the imperial theme.

> (I.iii.127–129)

But the imagined act of murder swells in his mind until it is too big for its place, and his heart beats as if it were choking in its chamber.

> Why do I yield to that suggestion
> Whose horrid image doth unfix my hair
> And make my seated heart knock at my ribs,
> Against the use of nature? Present fears
> Are less than horrible imaginings.
> My thought, whose murder yet is but fantastical,
> Shakes so my single state of man that function
> Is smother'd in surmise, and nothing is
> But what is not.

> (I.iii.134–142)

Meanwhile Lady Macbeth at home is visited by no such fears. When the crisis comes she will break sooner than her husband does, but her brittleness then will mean the same thing that her melodrama means now: she is a slighter person than Macbeth, has a poorer imagination, and holds in her mind less of that power which enables it to stand up under torture. The news that Duncan is coming to her house inspires her to pray that her blood be made thick; for the theme of thickness is so far not terrible in her thought.

> Come, thick night,
> And pall thee in the dunnest smoke of hell,
> That my keen knife see not the wound it makes,
> Nor heaven peep through the blanket of the dark
> To cry, "Hold, hold!"

> (I.v.51–55)

The blanket of the dark—it seems to her an agreeable image, and by no means suggests an element that can enwrap or smother. With Macbeth it is different; his soliloquy in the seventh scene shows him occupied with images of nets and tangles: the consequences of Duncan's death may coil about him like an endless rope.

> If it were done when 't is done, then 't were well
> It were done quickly. If the assassination
> Could trammel up the consequence, and catch
> With his surcease success; that but this blow
> Might be the be-all and the end-all here,
> But here, upon this bank and shoal of time,
> We'd jump the life to come. But in these cases
> We still have judgement here, that we but teach
> Bloody instructions, which, being taught, return
> To plague the inventor.

> > (I.vii.1–10)

A WORLD OF TERROR

And his voice rises to shrillness as he broods in terror upon the endless echo which such a death may make in the world.

> His virtues
> Will plead like angels, trumpet-tongu'd, against
> The deep damnation of his taking-off;
> And pity, like a naked new-born babe
> Striding the blast, or heaven's cherubin hors'd
> Upon the sightless couriers of the air,
> Shall blow the horrid deed in every eye,
> That tears shall drown the wind.

> > (I.vii.18–25)

It is terror such as this that Lady Macbeth must endeavor to allay in what is after all a great mind. Her scolding cannot do so. She has commanded him to screw his courage to the sticking-point, but what is the question that haunts him when he comes from Duncan's bloody bed, with hands that can never be washed white again?

> Wherefore could not I pronounce "Amen"?
> I had most need of blessing, and "Amen"
> Stuck in my throat.

> > (II.ii.31–33)

He must not consider such things so deeply, his lady warns him. But he does, and in good time she will follow suit. That same night the Scottish earth, shaking in a convincing sympathy as the Roman earth in "Julius Caesar" never shook, considers the grievous state of a universe that suffocates in the breath of its own history. Lamentings are heard in the air, strange screams of death, and prophecies of dire combustion and confused events (II.iii.61–63). And the next morning, says Ross to an old man he meets,

By the clock 't is day,
And yet dark night strangles the travelling lamp.

(II.iv.6–7)

Macbeth is now king, but his fears "stick deep" in Banquo (II.i.50). The thought of one more murder that will give him perhaps the "clearness" he requires (III.i.133) seems for a moment to free his mind from its old obsessive horror of dust and thickness, and he can actually invoke these conditions—in the only verse he ever uses with conscious literary intention.

> Come, seeling night,
> Scarf up the tender eye of pitiful day,
> And with thy bloody and invisible hand
> Cancel and tear to pieces that great bond
> Which keeps me pale! Light thickens, and the crow
> Makes wing to the rooky wood;
> Good things of day begin to droop and drowse,
> While night's black agents to their preys do rouse.

(III.ii.46–53

The melodrama of this, and its inferiority of effect, may warn us that Macbeth is only pretending to hope. The news of Fleance's escape brings him at any rate his fit again, and he never more ceases to be "cabin'd, cribb'd, confin'd" (III.iv.24). He is caught in the net for good, his feet have sunk into quicksand from which they cannot be freed, his bosom like Lady Macbeth's is "stuff'd" with "perilous stuff which weighs upon the heart" (V.iii.44–45)—the figure varies, but the theme does not. A strange world not wholly of his own making has closed around him and rendered him motionless. His gestures are spasmodic at the end, like those of one who knows he is hopelessly engulfed. And every metaphor he uses betrays his belief that the universal congestion is past cure:

> What rhubarb, senna, or what purgative drug,
> Would scour these English hence?

(V.iii.55–56)

The answer is none. . . .

TIME HAS GONE AWRY

Another element has gone awry, and it is one so fundamental to man's experience that Shakespeare has given it a central position among those symbols which express the disintegration of the hero's world. Time is out of joint, inoperative, dissolved. "The time has been," says Macbeth, when he could fear; and "the time has been" that when the brains were out a man would die, and there an end (III.iv.78–80). The repetition reveals that Macbeth is haunted by a sense that time has slipped its grooves; it flows wild and formless through his world, and is the deep cause of all the anomalies that terrify him. Certain of these anomalies are local or specific: the bell that rings on the night of the murder, the knocking at the gate. . . . But other anomalies are general, and these are the worst. The words of Banquo to the witches:

> If you can look into the seeds of time,
> And say which grain will grow and which will not,
>
> (I.iii.58–59)

plant early in the play a conception of time as something which fulfills itself by growing—and which, the season being wrong, can swell to monstrous shape. . . .

Macbeth's speech when he comes back from viewing Duncan's body may have been rehearsed and is certainly delivered for effect; yet he best knows what the terms signify:

> Had I but died an hour before this chance,
> I had liv'd a blessed time; for, from this instant,
> There's nothing serious in mortality.
>
> (II.iii.96–98)

He has a premonition even now of time's disorders; of his own premature descent into the sere,[2] the yellow leaf (V.iii.23); of his failure like any other man to

> pay his breath
> To time and mortal custom.
>
> (IV.i.99–100)

"What, will the line stretch out to the crack of doom?" he cries when Banquo's eight sons appear to him in the witches' cavern (IV.i.117). Time makes sense no longer; its proportions are strange, its content meaningless. For Lady Macbeth in her mind's disease the minutes have ceased to march in their true file and order; her sleep-walking soliloquy (V.i) recapitulates the play, but there is no temporal design among the fragments of the past—the blood, the body of Duncan, the fears of her husband, the ghost of Banquo, the slaughter of Lady Macduff, the ringing of the bell, and again the blood—which float detached from one another in her memory. And for Macbeth time has become

2. dry, withered

> a tale
> Told by an idiot, full of sound and fury,
> Signifying nothing.

(V.v.26–28)

Death is dusty, and the future is a limitless desert of tomorrows. His reception of the news that Lady Macbeth has died is like nothing else of a similar sort in Shakespeare. . . . But Macbeth, drugged beyond feeling, supped full with horrors, and tired of nothing so much as of coincidence in calamity, can only say in a voice devoid of tone:

> She should have died hereafter;
> There would have been a time for such a word.

(V.v.17–18)

There would, that is, if there were such a thing as time. Then such words as "died" and "hereafter" would have their meaning. Not now, however, for time itself has died. . . .

FINALLY, GOODNESS BREAKS IN

Scotland may seem to have become the grave of men and not their mother (IV.iii.166); death and danger may claim the whole of that bleeding country; but there is another country to the south where a good king works miracles with his touch. The rest of the world is what it always was; time goes on; events stretch out through space in their proper forms. Shakespeare again has enclosed his evil within a universe of good, his storm center within wide areas of peace. And from this outer world Malcolm and Macduff will return to heal Scotland of its ills. Their conversation in London before the pious Edward's palace (IV.iii) is not an interruption of the play; it is one of its essential parts, glancing forward as it does to a conclusion wherein Macduff can say, "The time is free" (V.viii.55), and wherein Malcolm can promise that deeds of justice, "planted newly with the time," will be performed "in measure, time, and place" (V.viii.64–73). Malcolm speaks the language of the play, but he has recovered its lost idiom. Blood will cease to flow, movement will recommence, fear will be forgotten, sleep will season every life, and the seeds of time will blossom in due order. The circle of safety which Shakespeare has drawn around his central horror is thinly drawn, but it is finely drawn and it holds.

Macbeth: A Study in Fear

Lily B. Campbell

Lily B. Campbell argues that Macbeth and Lady Macbeth are undone by fear rather than ambition. It is this fear that results in false courage and leads to their killing of Duncan. According to Campbell, Lady Macbeth is more passionate, Macbeth both more imaginative and rational; consequently, they display false courage differently, they respond differently to fear, and they come to different ends. Lily B. Campbell, who taught at the University of California at Los Angeles, has written extensively on Elizabethan literature. She is the author of *Scenes and Machines on the English Stage* and *Shakespeare's "Histories"; Mirrors of Elizabethan Policy.*

[*Macbeth*] is really a study in fear. And since fear is but one of a pair of passions, Shakespeare, according to his habit, paints the passion studied against the background of its opposite. . . . Bryskett[1] called them fury and fear. But however they were named, they are the passions which represent the excess and the defect of the virtuous mean[2] which was known generally as fortitude or courage or strength. Wylkinson[3] translated Aristotle:

> feare & folyshe [foolish] hardinesse corrupteth the valiantnes of man, for whi? the fearefull fleeth from everye thyng. And the hardye assaileth every thyng, beleving in himselfe to bring it to passe. . . .

ARISTOTLE'S DEFINITION OF FALSE COURAGE

Defining fortitude as "a meane betwene feare and hardines", the *Ethiques* also explained in regard to false courage. . . .

It seems vague to conjecture where Shakespeare got his

1. Lodovico, in *Discourse of Civill Life* 2. middle; moderate position 3. John, translator of Aristotle's *Ethics*

special knowledge of this false courage, but in the various writers of his day who derived their analysis directly or indirectly from Aristotle these various sorts of specious courage were discussed: the civic courage resulting from the sense of shame; military courage; courage that came as ignorance of what was rightly to be feared; drunken courage; and the courage that is best described by Shakespeare in *Antony and Cleopatra:*

> To be furious,
> Is to be frighted out of fear; and in that mood
> The dove will peck the estridge.[4]

(III.xiii.195–97)

. . . It is with these various manifestations of that excess of fortitude, of which the defect is fear, that we have to do in the study of "brave Macbeth" and his lady. . . .

Aristotle stressed three things in his definition of fear: it is painful; it has to do with the future rather than the present; it arises from some mental picture of an evil that is painful or destructive. . . .

Aristotle further commented on the causes of our fear, listing many sorts of people whom we fear. He noted that we fear the enmity and anger of those who have power to do us harm; we fear injustice in the possession of power; we fear outraged virtue; we fear those who have us at their mercy, and therefore we fear those who share a secret with us lest they betray us; we fear those that have been wronged lest they seek retaliation; we fear those that have done wrong, since they stand in fear of retaliation; we fear those who have shown their power by destroying those stronger than we are; we fear those who are our rivals for something which we cannot both have at once. And the table stands as a pattern for the fears and murders and revenges of *Macbeth*. . . .

MACBETH AND LADY MACBETH DISPLAY EXCESSIVE COURAGE

Fear and courage are studied in the play as opposites, the defect and the excess of true fortitude. Ambition has no opposite and is here used without an opposite and is used only as a supplementary passion in any case. But passion is studied as it affects two different people especially—a man and a woman, Macbeth and Lady Macbeth.

In both Macbeth and Lady Macbeth there is seen the ambition which moves to rash deeds; in both there is seen the

4. **estridge:** hawk

gradual dissolution of fear, the one being led to final self-destruction, the other to the final fury of despair.

Yet it is of "brave Macbeth" that we first hear, for as I have said, the study of fear is placed against a background of its opposite. The bleeding captain tells of Macbeth, who is "Valour's minion", fighting Macdonwald,

> Till he unseam'd him from the nave to the chaps,
> And fix'd his head upon our battlements.

(I.ii.22–23)

Moreover, a fresh assault failed to dismay Banquo and Macbeth, so that the captain reports to Duncan:

> If I say sooth, I must report they were
> As cannons overcharg'd with double cracks; so they
> Doubly redoubled strokes upon the foe.
> Except they meant to bathe in reeking wounds,
> Or memorize another Golgotha,[5]
> I cannot tell.

(I.ii.36–41)

Macbeth is, indeed, "Bellona's bridegroom",[6] though critics seem rather at a loss to know just who Bellona's bridegroom may have been. At any rate, we have pictured at the outset the military courage which in the captain's report seems bloody and rash and definitely pictured as an excess of fortitude, and which may well be ranked as one of the types specially listed by Aristotle as false courage.

In the next scene it is, however, a very different Macbeth who, with Banquo, meets the three witches on the blasted heath in the thunder that appropriately heralds the appearance of the supernatural on the stage. Now it is Banquo who boldly challenges the witches, while Macbeth can but feebly echo his question to them. . . . It is necessary to note carefully that this scene emphasizes from the beginning, therefore, the fear that appears in Macbeth just as his rash military courage appeared in the preceding scene. And this fear still holds him as the witches reply to Banquo in the final oracular:

> Thou shalt get kings, though thou be none;

(I.iii.67)

. . . we see Lady Macbeth in the scene which follows reading her lord's letter in which he tells her of the witches' prophecies and of their strange fulfilment, not failing to mention that he stood rapt with the wonder of it, we hear her

---

5. **Golgotha:** the "Place of a Skull" where Christ was crucified 6. **Bellona's bridegroom:** the mate of the goddess of war

but emphasize this conflict of fear and ambition that must always characterize Macbeth. But she embroiders her theme:

> Yet do I fear thy nature;
> It is too full o' the milk of human kindness
> To catch the nearest way. Thou wouldst be great,
> Art not without ambition, but without
> The illness should attend it. What thou wouldst highly,
> That wouldst thou holily; wouldst not play false,
> And yet wouldst wrongly win. . . .

(I.iv.17–23)

LADY MACBETH CONTROLS MACBETH'S DOUBTS

With Duncan as his guest in his castle, Macbeth starts to argue the deed in his mind. . . . This deep fear of heaven's justice, of the unknown decrees of justice, of retribution in the now, as well as in the hereafter, is but the prologue to Macbeth's argument. . . .

But Lady Macbeth will have nothing of such temporizing. Her taunts again centre about the same question of fear and ambition:

> Art thou afeard
> To be the same in thine own act and valour
> As thou art in desire? . . .

(I.vii.39–41)

Was he then less than man, a beast, when he proposed the enterprise? Rather he was then a man, and to be more would be to be more than man. Time and place, then wanting, now make themselves. And again she argues on the basis of her sex, as before; she would as a mother have killed her child at her breast rather than to have failed in such an oath as he has sworn. And to Macbeth's timid,

> If we should fail ?

she replies passionately:

> We fail!
> But screw your courage to the sticking-place,
> And we'll not fail.

(I.vii.59–61)

It is she who plans the deed—the drunken chamberlains, the death of Duncan, the guilt laid on others. . . .

But in his admiration he [Macbeth] has not forgotten fear, and he questions the surety with which the guilt may be attached to the chamberlains. Then at last, at the close of the act, he utters his determination in which the resolve of ambition is seen brought to the courage that is the fear of shame and is, indeed, a fearful courage:

> I am settled, and bend up[7]
> Each corporal agent to this terrible feat.
>
> (I.vii.79–80)

BOTH LADY MACBETH AND MACBETH DISPLAY FEAR

. . . The next scene reveals the first sign of fear in Lady Macbeth, for her admission that she would herself have killed Duncan had he not resembled her father as he sleptis an admission of weakness she would earlier have scorned. Moreover, her courage now is admittedly the sort of false courage listed by Aristotle as achieved by drink, for she says:

> That which hath made them drunk hath made me bold;
> What hath quench'd them hath given me fire.
>
> (II.ii.1–2)

But as the terror-stricken Macbeth comes from doing the deed with his fearful whimperings about the grooms' "Amen" and "God bless us", she answers prophetically:

> These deeds must not be thought
> After these ways; so, it will make us mad.
>
> (II.ii.33–34)

It is then that Macbeth introduces the theme of sleep which is always found in any study of fear, and he speaks again by the book:

> Methought I heard a voice cry, "Sleep no more!
> Macbeth does murder sleep,"—the innocent sleep,
> Sleep that knits up the ravell'd sleave of care. . . .
>
> (II.ii.35–37)

But Lady Macbeth reproves him for his "brainsickly" talking about these things. Her fear is more active and more provident. She will have him wash his hands; she will have him carry back the daggers to the King's chamber and smear the grooms with blood.

Macbeth is fearful beyond care, however:

> I'll go no more.
> I am afraid to think what I have done;
> Look on 't again I dare not
>
> (II.ii.50–52)

And Lady Macbeth with her chiding "Infirm of purpose!" goes to the practical task of smearing the grooms with blood, while Macbeth can but look at his hands and wonder at the

7. **bend up:** stretch tight as a strung bow

endless red of the blood thereon as the loud knocking commences. . . .

It must be noted that while these first two acts of the play are taken up with the struggle of two passions for victory, while that struggle has been resolved by the deed which fear was not quite able to keep ambition from accomplishing, yet in the very moment when ambition seems to have won, fear has in reality taken possession of the victim. After the murder of Duncan, the whole play is motivated by the increasing passion of fear. . . .

Act V presents swiftly and relentlessly the results of passion, of the passion which has become mortal sin. First it is Lady Macbeth that we see enduring the fate of the sinful in whom fear and remorse have already begun to effect the punishment for evil. That Shakespeare chose to manifest Lady Macbeth's melancholy as a disturbance in her sleep shows that he was a student of the moral philosophy of the time, for as we have seen earlier, all the accounts of fear are concerned with the effect of fear on sleep. Macbeth's own cry, "Macbeth hath murdered sleep" was but the statement of the realized truth of philosophy. . . .

THE EFFECTS ON LADY MACBETH

But Lady Macbeth's sleep has been troubled as only the sleep of those can be troubled who have been led by passion into melancholy, whose minds have become "infected minds". She walks and talks in her sleep. Thus Nashe[8] explained in accordance with the popular belief of the day that we make for ourselves "images of memory" and some superfluous humour in the night erects a puppet stage for these images. It is thus that Lady Macbeth shows the images of memory which have been most deeply etched by fear. She sees the spot of blood which will not out. She sees again the murdered Duncan. Yet who would have thought the old man to have had so much blood in him? She recalls Lady Macduff. She recalls her husband's dangerous starting. She smells blood still. She remembers her fearful admonition to Macbeth on the night of the murder to put on his nightgown, on the night of the feast to put away his imagination of Banquo's ghost. Then it is the knocking at the gate that she hears again.

Anyone who does not believe that Lady Macbeth as well as her husband is the victim of fear should study these im-

8. Thomas, in *Terrors of the Night*

ages of memory, for they reveal horror and fear. She does not dwell upon the havoc wrought by such deeds; she rather recalls those images associated with her extreme moments of terror and fear: the blood upon her hands, her husband's starting that endangered all, the old man bleeding so much blood, the feast marred by Banquo's ghost, and then the awful knocking that summoned fear on the night of Duncan's murder. All this is not remorse but fear. And in the last act we see the pitiful results of the fear that conquered finally the reason that so long held it in abeyance. It was long before Lady Macbeth's reason gave way before the reiterated fears of her imperial ascent, but at last passion has conquered reason fully, it would seem.[9] Furthermore, it must be noted that even as Macbeth revealed his guilt at the feast to those who were his guests, so Lady Macbeth finally revealed her guilt to the watchers. It is thus that the old themes of tragedy are newly spoken by Shakespeare. And it is the theme of moral philosophy which is spoken as well in the doctor's words:

> More needs she the divine than the physician.
>
> (V.i.82)

THE EFFECTS ON MACBETH

In the next scenes we turn again to Macbeth. . . . As the servant enters to tell of the oncoming host, Macbeth rages at him, calling him "lily-liver'd boy" and "whey-face" and bidding him "over-red" his fear. But in a moment of realization he becomes sad, counting the things fit for age which are not for him. He speaks truly when he says:

> I am sick at heart.
>
> (V.iii.19)

But as he turns to fevered activity, the doctor reports concerning Lady Macbeth. . . . And at the news of the death of the Queen he has scarcely time to rail at life in the great speech ending with the final estimate of life:

> It is a tale
> Told by an idiot, full of sound and fury,
> Signifying nothing.
>
> (V.v.26–28)

As the theorists of fear have pointed out, there cannot be

---

9. From the first of the play, Lady Macbeth's reason was subdued by passion. Passion determined the end. Reason but determined the means to that end. Now Reason no longer functions at all. Passion reigns alone.

fear where we have experienced every horror already; there is some hope necessary to fear. But from this point on, we see Macbeth who has "supp'd full with horrors", advancing to that despair which is the final stage of fear and which manifests itself as fury. On the news of the death of the Queen there follows fast the news of the advance of Birnam wood. And Macbeth advances to defend his castle with his thoughts full of the witches and their promise, furiously crying:

> Ring the alarum-bell! Blow, wind! come, wrack!
> At least we'll die with harness on our back.
>
> (V.v.51–52)

When next we see Macbeth in battle, he reasons concerning his fortune:

> They have tied me to a stake; I cannot fly,
> But, bear-like, I must fight the course. What's he
> That was not born of woman? Such a one
> Am I to fear, or none.
>
> (V.vii.1-4)

The Macbeth here is the Macbeth of the first scenes of the play, the Macbeth in military action, the Macbeth who recalls the "brave Macbeth" with which the play opened. But here again he fights irrationally, not with the fortitude of the man controlling his passion by reason, but rather with the courage of the animal that fights without reason when there is no choice but to fight for its life. Shakespeare could not say more clearly that this apparent courage is that of the beast and not of the man.

But Macbeth's final ground for hope is taken away. Just as the advance of Birnam wood has made him doubt the assurance of the witches, so now the parley with Macduff in the next stage of the battle makes it apparent that their warning to beware Macduff and their promise that Macbeth should not yield to one of woman born are not irreconcilable. To Macduff's statement concerning his birth, Macbeth replies:

> Accursed be that tongue that tells me so,
> For it hath cow'd my better part of man!
>
> (V.viii.17–18)

And as he renounces faith in the witches, he cries in despair, "I'll not fight with thee".

But as Macduff calls him coward and demands that he yield, he cries again in utter despair:

> I will not yield,

> To kiss the ground before young Malcolm's feet
> And to be baited with the rabble's curse.
> Though Birnam wood be come to Dunsinane,
> And thou oppos'd being of no woman born,
> Yet I will try the last.

(V.viii.27–32)

The entrance of Macduff with Macbeth's head comes as evidence of the final end of the "dead butcher" who was Macbeth, and we hear from the newly proclaimed King of the end also of "the fiend-like queen":

> Who, as 't is thought, by self and violent hands
> Took off her life.

(V.viii.70–71)

According to this analysis, then, *Macbeth* is a study in the complementary pair of passions of rash courage and fear. It begins with the courage that is not real courage and ends with the courage that is not real courage. It pictures in turn the military courage of Macbeth, his excited valour and excessive bravery in action, the drunken courage of Lady Macbeth, the bravery of passion, the fury of despair, and the courage of desperation. It pictures as well superstitious fear, melancholy fear, the fear of those who share our secrets, the fear of those who are our rivals, the fear of those whom we have harmed, all the fears that lead to murder after murder, that result in melancholy, in sleeplessness, in disturbing dreams, in ghosts and visions, in fits of passion, in frenzy, in sleep-walking, in self-destruction; fears that destroy peace and happiness and honour and hope; fears that make ambition fruitless and success a mockery.

THE WILL TO DO EVIL

But the study is also a study of man and woman. Lady Macbeth is pictured as sinning partly, I think, in that she is false to herself as woman. She is pictured as consciously unsexing herself, as converting all that is womanly into the courage and determination to be cruel. Even more than Macbeth, she wills to do evil. She dyes her will in her ambition. Because her will is strong and directed by passion and not by reason, the fear that is her punishment is more terrible than that of Macbeth and brings her even to the despairful sin of self-destruction.

Macbeth is, however, not only a study of fear; it is a study in fear. The sounds and images in the play combine to give the atmosphere of terror and fear. The incantation of the witches, the bell that tolls while Duncan dies, the cries of Duncan, the cries of the women as Lady Macbeth dies, the owl, the knocking at the gate, the wild horses that ate each other, the storm, the quaking of the earth—all of these are the habitual accompaniments of the wilfully fearful in literature.

Life-Enhancing Themes in *Macbeth*

G. Wilson Knight

G. Wilson Knight focuses on life-enhancing themes juxtaposed with those of evil and destruction. Knight cites four themes of this kind: the honor of warriors, the magnificence of kingship, sleep and feasting, and nature in its purity. At the end of the play, Knight shows, creation and life-giving forces replace destruction. G. Wilson Knight was professor emeritus of English literature at the University of Leeds in England and chancellors' professor of English at Trinity College, Toronto. He is the author of books on poetry, religion, Shakespeare, and several other British poets; among his titles are *The Wheel of Fire, Shakespeare and Religion,* and *Poets of Action.*

The opposition of life and death forces is strong in *Macbeth.* Here we find the dark and evil negation endued with a positive strength, successfully opposing things of health and life. Elsewhere I have discussed the evil: here I give a primary attention to the life-themes it opposes. They are: (i) Warrior-honour, (ii) Imperial magnificence, (iii) Sleep and Feasting, and (iv) Ideas of creation and nature's innocence. . . .

THE THEME OF WARRIOR-HONOUR

Fear is at the heart of this play. Now, if we consider the beginning and ending too, we find a very clear rhythm of courage, fear, and courage. The play ends on a note of courage. Macbeth is from the first a courageous soldier. His warrior-honour is emphasized. He is 'brave Macbeth' (I.ii.16), 'valour's minion' (I.ii.19), 'Bellona's bridegroom'[1] (I.ii.54), 'noble Macbeth' (I.ii.67). Duncan exclaims:

O valiant cousin! worthy gentleman!

(I.ii.24)

1. **Bellona's bridegroom:** the mate of the goddess of war

Reprinted from G. Wilson Knight, *The Imperial Theme: Further Interpretation of Shakespeare's Tragedies, Including the Roman Plays* (Oxford: Oxford University Press, 1931).

He is 'a peerless kinsman' (I.iv.58)—the Duncan-Macbeth relationship is always stressed. Courage in war is a thing of 'honour' (I.ii.44). So Macbeth is rewarded for his valour by a title, earnest of an even greater 'honour' (I.iii.104). . . .

Throughout thoughts of the family (especially childhood), clan, or nation are associated here. All are units of peace, concord, life. All are twined with 'honour'. So the subject is bound to his lord by love and honour. The value of warrior-ship may not be dissociated from allegiance: it is one with the ideal of kingship and imperial power. . . .

Sons, kinsmen, thanes—all are bound close together. Scotland is a family, Duncan its head. A natural law binds all degrees in proper place and allegiance. Only in terms of this allegiance is courage an honourable ideal. Observe, too, how the king's 'honours' are compared to 'stars', the king's gentle rule of love thus blending with the universal lights. But the evil that grips Macbeth must hide from such things of brilliance and universal beauty:

> Stars, hide your fires;
> Let not light see my black and deep desires:
> The eye wink[2] at the hand; yet let that be,
> Which the eye fears, when it is done, to see.

> (I.iv.50)

. . . Yet Lady Macbeth wins largely by appealing to Macbeth's 'valour' (I.vii.40). If he now fails in courage, she will henceforth despise equally his courage and his love (I.vii.39): warriorship and love being ever close in Shakespeare, either in contrast or association. . . .

Macbeth at the last, by self-knowledge, attains grace. He knows that he must forfeit 'honour' and all things of concord and life:

> . . . that which should accompany old age,
> As honour, love, obedience, troops of friends,
> I must not look to have. . . .

> (V.iii.24)

These are the social realities he has desecrated by his fear-some rule. A rule of fear. Fear is here our dominant emotion. Not only Macbeth—all are paralysed by fear during the middle action. At the start, we saw courage, unity, honour, under the gracious rule of Duncan. But the valour of Scotland is temporarily smothered by evil. When at the end security and peace return, the contrast is marked by Siward's words

---

2. **wink**: shut; i.e., be blind to what I do

on his son, who 'has paid a soldier's debt' (V.vii.68), and died 'like a man' (V.vii. 72). . . . So we see courage desecrated by evil and fear, then at the end courage—in Macbeth or young Siward—victorious. . . .

THE THEME OF IMPERIAL MAGNIFICENCE

This warrior-theme is closely twined with our next positive value: imperial magnificence. On the ethical—as opposed to the metaphysical—plane, Macbeth fails through trying to advance from deserved honour as a noble thane to the higher kingly honour to which he has no rights. . . .

Macbeth and his wife reach out for power and glory: the sense-forms correspondent are crowns and sceptres. The glint of these burns grimly and sullenly through the murk. Lady Macbeth would drive from her lord

> All that impedes thee from the golden round,
> Which fate and metaphysical[3] aid doth seem
> To haze thee crown'd withal.
>
> (I.v.29)

The 'golden round': solid, glorious gold to bind the brow with royalty. The same glinting solidity burns in the phrase-ology, especially the final word, of:

> Which shall to all our nights and days to come
> Give solely sovereign sway and masterdom.
>
> (I.v.70)

These things are, as it were, the finest flower of world-honour, the sweetest prizes of life. They are glorious things of life. So she presses him on to win the 'ornament of life' (I.vii.42), though Macbeth objects to this absurd grasping of additional royalty by a man royally honoured already. He would wear his 'golden opinions' in 'their newest gloss' rather than risk losing them so soon (I.vii.32). So Macbeth sees clearly that the gold of evil desire will add nothing to his real honour: yet he cannot resist. . . .

Outward royalty is, by itself, a nothing in comparison with nature's kingliness:

> Our fears in Banquo
> Stick deep; and in his royalty of nature
> Reigns that which would be fear'd . . .
>
> (III.i.49)

So he fears, envies, hates Banquo who has the reality of ho-nour whereas he has but a mockery, a ghoulish dream of

3. **metaphysical:** supernatural

royalty. . . . He has grasped these gold power-symbols to himself: and they are utterly 'barren' in every sense; barren of joy and content, barren of posterity. So falsely has Macbeth made himself the centre and end of all things: a 'fruitless' philosophy. To this the evil has tricked him. . . .

Macbeth's evil is a lust, like unruly love; a centring of reality in the self. A turning-inward of the mind and its purposes, an obsession with the solitary self unharmonized with wider considerations. So he sells his 'eternal jewel' (III.i.68) for the riches and glory of unrighteous kingship. 'Jewels' may thus suggest spiritual or earthly riches here, as elsewhere in Shakespeare. . . .

The evil is opposed to the supreme glory of kingship. In blood-imagery, the two curiously blend: sensuous glory with horror. The evil smear of dull red becomes twice a brilliant gold:

I'll gild[4] the faces of the grooms withal;
For it must seem their guilt.

(II.ii.56)

and,

Here lay Duncan,
His silver skin lac'd with his golden blood,[5]
And his gash'd stabs looked like a breach in nature
For ruin's wasteful entrance.

(II.iii.117)

THE THEMES OF SLEEPING AND FEASTING

. . . So much for Macbeth's insecure tenure of imperial magnificence. Now I pass to the even more fundamental ideas of 'sleep', 'feasting', and 'nature'. Sleep and feasting are important. Peaceful sleep is often disturbed by nightmare; this I have observed elsewhere. Here we may observe how closely 'sleep' is twined with 'feasting'. Both are creative, restorative, forces of nature. So Macbeth and his Queen are reft of both during the play's action. Feasting and sleep are twin life-givers:

Methought I heard a voice cry, 'Sleep no more!
Macbeth does murder sleep', the innocent sleep,
Sleep that knits up the ravell'd sleave[6] of care,
The death of each day's life, sore labour's bath,
Balm of hurt minds, great nature's second course,
Chief nourisher in life's feast—

(II.ii.36)

---

4. **gild:** a grim pun; Shakespeare's contemporaries often confused red and gold 5. **laced . . . blood:** overlaid with blood as a garment is ornamented with gold 6. **ravell'd sleave:** tangled skein

The retributive suffering is apt. Macbeth murdered Duncan in sleep, after feasting him. . . . Because he murdered hospitality and sleep, therefore his punishment is a living death, without peaceful sleep or peaceful feeding:

> But let the frame of things disjoint, both the worlds suffer,[7]
> Ere we will eat our meal in fear, and sleep
> In the affliction of these terrible dreams
> That shake us nightly . . .

> (III.ii.16)

. . . Now the evil-feasting opposition is powerful here. Duncan compares his joy in Macbeth's success to a banquet:

> True, worthy Banquo; he is full so valiant;
> And in his commendations I am fed;
> It is a banquet to me.

> (I.iv.54)

Macbeth's honourable prowess is a life-bringing food to Duncan, to Scotland. Lady Macbeth's hospitality to Duncan is emphasized: she is his 'honoured hostess' (I.vi.10), his 'fair and noble hostess' (I.vi.24). She and Macbeth entertain him with a fine feast:

> *Hautboys and torches. Enter a Sewer, and divers Servants*
> *with dishes and service, and pass over the stage.*

> (I.vii)

Feasting and music: a usual grouping of effects. . . . Duncan, wearied by 'his day's hard journey' (I.vii.62), goes to his chamber to sleep 'soundly' (I.vii.63), after having distributed his bounty to his hosts: he is 'in unusual pleasure' and 'shut up in measureless content' (II.i.13–17). . . .

After the murder, feasting is again emphasized. It is shown how

> . . . this even-handed justice
> Commends the ingredients of our poisoned chalice
> To our own lips.

> (I.vii.10)

Macbeth finds he has 'put rancours in the vessel of' his 'peace' (III.i.67). He may not feast with his lords in peace and harmony. Banquo's ghost breaks into the attempted festivity, disperses it, throws it into disorder. At the start, hospitality, conviviality, 'welcome' and 'degree' are emphasized: the very things Macbeth has so brutally desecrated.

> *MACBETH.* You know your own degrees; sit down: at first
> And last the hearty welcome.

---

7. **let . . . suffer:** let heaven and earth perish

LORDS.   Thanks to your majesty.
MACBETH. Ourself will mingle with society,
And play the humble host.
Our hostess keeps her state,[8] but in best time
We will require her welcome.
LADY MACBETH. Pronounce it for me, sir, to all our friends;
For my heart speaks they are welcome.
MACBETH. See, they encounter thee with their hearts' thanks.
Both sides are even: here I'll sit i' the midst:
Be large in mirth; anon we'll drink a measure
The table round.

(III.iv.I)

Hospitality is bounteous. . . .

[*LADY MACBETH:*] To feed were best at home;
From thence the sauce to meat is ceremony;
Meeting were bare without it.
MACBETH.   Sweet remembrancer!
Now, good digestion wait on appetite,
And health on both!

(III.iv.35)

'Digestion', 'health', 'sauce', 'meat'. Against this life-force of feasting, conviviality, social friendliness and order, comes a death, a ghost, smashing life-forms with phantasms of evil and guilt: an unreality, a 'nothing', like the air-drawn dagger, creating chaos of order and reality, dispersing the social unit. . . .

After the Ghost's disappearance Macbeth recovers, again speaks words of 'love', 'health', and friendly communion:

Come, love and health to all;
Then I'll sit down. Give me some wine; fill full.
I drink to the general joy o' the whole table,
And to our dear friend Banquo, whom we miss;
Would he were here! to all, and him, we thirst,
And all to all.

(III.iv.87)

The Ghost reappears. . . . Death, destruction, chaos—these are the forms of evil opposed to the lifejoys of feast and friendship, and all social concord.

The three outstanding scenes of the middle action all illustrate the evil-feasting opposition. First there is Duncan's murder in sleep and after elaborate feasting by his host, kinsman, and subject: all concepts which stress Macbeth's ruthless desecration of social units of human life. Next, we find Banquo's ghost violently forbidding that Macbeth enjoy that hospitality and feasting which he has desecrated. Our third scene is that

---

8. **Keeps . . . state:** i.e., sits on her throne apart

with the Weird Sisters in their cavern. The contrast with the banquet scene is vivid. Here we watch a devils'-banqueting, the Weird Women with their cauldron and its holocaust of hideous ingredients. The banquet-idea has been inverted. Instead of suggesting health, this one is brewed to cause 'toil and trouble'. . . . The ingredients suggest an absolute indigestibility. It is a parody of banqueting, a death-banquet, a 'hell-broth' (IV.i.19). It is all quite meaningless, nameless, negative, utterly black:

> MACBETH. How now, you secret, black and midnight hags!
> What is 't you do?
> THE WEIRD WOMEN. A deed without a name.

> (IV.i.48)

THE THEME OF NATURE

. . . The Cauldron Scene, with its disjected members of animal and human bodies, and also its prophecies relating to 'nature', suggests a yet wider view of the opposition active throughout *Macbeth*. The *Macbeth*-evil attacks honour and imperial magnificence, life-forms of feeding, health, society: it also decisively attacks 'nature'. Nature in its purity is clearly another 'life' theme, only one degree removed from 'feasting'. But nature is seldom apparent here in purity and grace: when it is, that appearance is important. Nature-references blend with human themes, especially in point of procreation and childhood. . . .

We are confronted usually by a nature-distortion, a reality essentially unnatural, all but unreal. Most of the nature here is therefore an impossible, an unnatural nature. There are, however, a few suggestions of nature in her native integrity and beauty. . . .

Nature's creative beauty is remarked by Banquo:

> DUNCAN. This castle hath a pleasant seat;[9] the air
> Nimbly and sweetly recommends itself
> Unto our gentle senses.
> BANQUO.   This guest of summer,
> The temple-haunting martlet,[10] does approve,[11]
> By his loved mansionry, that the heaven's breath
> Smells wooingly here: no jutty, frieze,
> Buttress, nor coign of vantage,[12] but this bird
> Hath made his pendent bed and procreant cradle:
> Where they most breed and haunt, I have observ'd,
> The air is delicate.

> (I.vi.1.)

9. **seat:** situation 10. **martlet:** a species of swallow which builds for her nest a little round mud cell under the eaves of the roof 11. **approve:** demonstrate 12. **coign of vantage:** convenient corner

Notice the strong emphasis on 'senses', 'wooing', and 'delicate' air; and the 'procreant cradle', the thought of 'breeding'. . . . Macbeth's crime is a blow against nature's unity and peace, a hideous desecration of all creative, family, and social duties, all union and concord: this is the bond he breaks, the 'great bond' that keeps him 'pale' (III.ii.49). . . .

Nature's food of 'milk' is often mentioned in this connexion. Lady Macbeth fears her lord's 'nature': he is 'too full o' the milk of human kindness' (I.v.17–18). She invokes spirits of evil to take her own 'milk for gall' (I.v.49). Then, boasting of her conquest over natural pity, she speaks the terrible lines:

> . . . I have given suck, and know
> How tender 'tis to love the babe that milks me:
> I would, while it was smiling in my face,
> Have pluck'd my nipple from his boneless gums,
> And dash'd the brains out, had I so sworn as you
> Have done to this.

(I.vii.54)

The child-thought is frequent. There is the unnatural horror of the 'birth-strangled babe' (IV.i.30), and the matter of Macduff's mysterious birth. . . .

Innocent nature is in agony. Twice Macbeth is contrasted with a lamb (IV.iii,16—'a weak poor innocent lamb'; and IV. iii.54). Evil fear is contrasted with 'a summer's cloud' (III.iv.3) and 'good men's lives' die like 'flowers' (IV.iii.171). So nature will rise to avenge Macduff whose slaughtered wife and children demand redress. . . . Toward the close, nature's assistance is vividly apparent. Macbeth is 'ripe for shaking' (IV.iii.238). He himself knows it:

> I have lived long enough: my way of life
> Is fall'n into the sear, the yellow leaf . . .

(V.iii.22)

But the avenging forces are mostly young and fresh, to avenge the desecration of nature's childlike peace. . . .

Malcolm himself is compared to a flower dew-sprinkled: the Scottish lords would 'dew the sovereign flower and drown the weeds' (V.ii.30). So sweet a nature-image again suggests nature's assistance: which thought is even more clearly apparent in the matter of Birnam wood. Not a human army only attacks Dunsinane. The very trees rise against Macbeth, league with his enemies. That is creative nature accusing, asserting her strength after her long torment of destruction. So Birnam wood marches against Macbeth. . . .

As Macbeth's course becomes more reckless, the evil forces him to imprecate wholesale tempest and disorder on the universe. He would have the 'winds' untied, fighting against 'churches', swallowing up 'navigation', blowing down 'corn' and 'trees'; castles, palaces, pyramids, let all fall; he would let 'the treasure of nature's germens tumble all together' till destruction itself 'sicken' (IV.i.52–60). . . .

Lady Macbeth's sleep-walking is 'a great perturbation in nature' (V.i.10), for . . .

> unnatural deeds
> Do breed unnatural troubles . . .
>
>   (V.i.79)

It is a fitting culmination to this theme of dark and nightmare, evil which is set beyond any natural law of sense-contact:

> DOCTOR. You see, her eyes are open.
> GENTLEWOMAN. Ay, but their sense is shut.
>
>   (V.i.28)

So she walks, her body present but her consciousness beyond the imaginable universe pacing the lonely corridors of agonized remembrance in the other world of sleep. The play's action has been all along a waking nightmare: here nightmare usurps the powers allowed to waking life. . . .

I have regarded the evil in relation to life-forces. These may be divided as follows: (i) Human values, Warrior-honour and Imperial Sway; (ii) Human nature, sleep and feasting; (iii) Pure nature—animals, birds, winds, sun, and stars. Most important of all, we must observe the emergence of child-references. The negation here opposes all values, health, and nature: the creative process. Destruction is set against creation: hence our many references to mother's 'milk', the martlet's and wren's nest and young, to 'chickens', 'lambs', the strange use of 'egg' and 'fry' (IV.ii.84–5), and the child-themes. . . .

ULTIMATELY CREATION REPLACES DESTRUCTION

At the end youth comes armed against Macbeth. Birth opposes death. 'Issue' is an important word. Youth and babyhood oppose our evil. Macbeth murdered aged innocence and purity linked to the 'great office' (I.vii.18) of kingship. . . . He, who has placed his trust in chaos, hopes himself to 'live the lease of nature' (IV.i.99). But this joy is short-lived. . . . Too late he learns that to get kings is more blessed than to be king, creation more blessed than possession. For possession divorced from creation melts in the grasping hand: like flowers 'dying or ere they sicken' (IV.iii.173). . . . For Macbeth is childless, with a fruitless crown and barren sceptre, as evil is ever childless, unproductive. So he knows the process of life to hold no hope for him. It is merely a cruel catalogue of deaths strung together in time:

> To-morrow, and to-morrow, and to-morrow,
> Creeps in this petty pace from day to day
> To the last syllable of recorded time,
> And all our yesterdays have lighted fools
> The way to dusty death. Out, out, brief candle!
> Life 's but a walking shadow, a poor player
> That struts and frets his hour upon the stage
> And then is heard no more: it is a tale
> Told by an idiot, full of sound and fury,
> Signifying nothing.
>
> (V.v.19)

He sees all life from the death-aspect of time. And he is now himself reconciled to the 'nothing', the negation of evil and death. . . .

We see that disorder itself turns on disorder. So, too, the death-concept ever contradicts itself and becomes life to any intense contemplation. Absolute disorder prohibits self-consistency: it helps to slay itself. Death gives birth to life. Not nature alone, but 'both the worlds' (III.ii.16), natural and unnatural, life and death, come against Macbeth. . . .

In a final judgement the whole play may be writ down as a wrestling of destruction with creation: with sickening shock the phantasmagoria of death and evil are violently loosed on earth, and for a while the agony endures, destructive; there is a wrenching of new birth, itself disorderly and unnatural in this disordered world, and then creation's more firm-set sequent concord replaces chaos. The baby-peace is crowned.

The Supernatural Highlights the Play's Themes

Roy Walker

Roy Walker's close analysis of the two early scenes with the Witches establishes them as representatives of an independent supernatural element in the play. His explication of their lines and those of Macbeth and Banquo supports the notion that Macbeth, unlike Banquo, is susceptible to their temptations and will fulfill their riddling prophecy. Shakespearean critic Roy Walker is the author of *The Time Is out of Joint: A Study of* Hamlet.

Macbeth begins with an elemental convulsion. Thunder, Lightning, Rain. Only Shakespeare can convey the fury and significance of the Shakespearean tempest, as he did in *King Lear*, the tragedy that preceded *Macbeth:*

> Blow, winds, and crack your cheeks! rage! blow!
> You cataracts and hurricanoes, spout
> Till you have drench'd our steeples, drown'd the cocks!
> You sulphurous and thought-executing fires,
> Vaunt-couriers to oak-cleaving thunderbolts,
> Singe my white head! And thou, all-shaking thunder;
> Strike flat the thick rotundity o' the world!
> Crack nature's moulds, all germens spill at once
> That make ingrateful man!
>
> (Lear, III.ii.1–9)

At the beginning of *Macbeth* there is no human voice to interpret the meaning of the storm. Dimly we know that chaos wars against light. Hecate is creating an infernal trinity. Thunder, Lightning, Rain. From this vortex she whirls into existence Hecate's three hideous heads, three bodies, a triple curse upon humanity; sends her three phantoms to the world to dwell near blood of murdered men. . . . Flat white faces, withered and lifeless as the moon, black rags of chaos wildly blowing—

Reprinted from Roy Walker, *The Time Is Free: A Study of Macbeth* (London: Andrew Dakers, 1949).

When shall we three meet again
In Thunder, Lightning or in Rain?

(I.i.1–2)

THE WITCHES ESTABLISH THEIR
IDENTITY AND PURPOSE

The Witches' questions to each other and the answers
Hecate whispers to these three selves are crabbed and
crooked, as treacherously ambiguous as their own prophecies to men.

When the hurlyburly's done,
When the battle's lost and won,
That will be ere the set of sun.

(I.i.3–5)

They will dissolve back into the evil mystery when the storm
sinks. The end of the tempest is the end of the battle, lost and
won ere set of sun, lost by darkness and won by the god of
day. Hecate's battle is always lost, but not before blood has
flowed, confusion poured into the world through men
whose nature lies open to the storm of evil. Lost—and won.
The words have some such sinister meaning besides their
parallel reference to the Witches' task upon the earth.[1] There
a rebellion is bloodily repressed, invaders bloodily defeated,
and the victorious hero who bathed in reeking wounds has
yet unsatiated thoughts of blood. His battle too must be lost
and won ere set of sun; the battle of his own soul.

Where the place?
Upon the heath.
There to meet with Macbeth.

(I.i.6–7)

The Witches go to find a man who boasts he dares do all that
may become a man. An old prophetic saying [Jeremiah XVII,
5–6] stirs in the mind: 'cursed be the man that trusteth in
man, and maketh flesh his arm, and whose heart departeth
from the Lord. For he shall be like the heath in the desert,
and shall not see when good cometh; but shall inhabit the
parched places in the wilderness, in a salt land and not inhabited.' It is the road to dusty death.

I come, Graymalkin.
Paddock calls anon: Fair is foul and foul is fair

---

1. 'It is worth remembering that "Hurley-burley" implies more than "the tumult of
sedition or insurrection." Both it and "when the Battaile's lost, and wonne" suggest the
kind of metaphysical pitch-and-toss that is about to be played with good and evil.'—
L.C. Knight's *Explorations*, p. 18.

Hover through the fog and filthy air.

(I.i.8–11)

The Witches are guided by the things of darkness. Gray-malkin, the night-seeing cat, the nameless toad under the cold stone, whisper to the weird sisters perversion of the natural order: fair is foul, destroy it; foul is fair, nurture it. Hover through the fog and filthy air, how sweet it is when foul is fair! To the heath, sisters, to meet Macbeth who shall be like the heath and not see when good comes—or evil. In him already foul and fair conflict.

When they meet again upon the heath, heralded by thunder, the Witches have become practised in their black arts. Macbeth will hear a voice cry, 'Sleep no more,' and Lady Macbeth will rise in sleep to walk the night. Sleep, the Witches' enemy, is great nature's second course. They have power to disturb sleep:

> Sleep shall neither night nor day
> Hang upon his pent-house lid;
> He shall live a man forbid.
> Weary se'en-nights nine times nine,
> Shall he dwindle, peak, and pine:

(I.iii.19–23)

They can disturb the elements:

> I'll give thee a wind.
> Th' art kind.
> And I another.
> I myself have all the other.

(I.iii.11–14)

But though they can harass and disturb the sailor and raise the elements against him, they cannot themselves work his destruction. (As Juno loosed the tempests upon Aeneas[2] but could not destroy him as she wished.)

> Though his bark cannot be lost
> Yet it shall be tempest-tost.

(I.iii.24–25)

Nevertheless, ship and sailor may be both destroyed by storm, even if it is not in the Witches' power to doom them. Not only a sailor but a pilot may be killed (as Aeneas' pilot, Palinurus, was):

> Here I have a pilot's thumb,
> Wrack'd, as homeward he did come.

(I.iii.29–30)

---

2. Juno is the principal goddess of the Pantheon, the wife of Jupiter; Aeneas is the Trojan hero of Virgil's epic *Aeneid.*

MACBETH ARRIVES, IRONICALLY ECHOING THE WITCHES' WORDS

No sooner are the words uttered than the echoing and re-echoing sound of the drum is heard. Macbeth is approaching! Great ships and their unsuspecting pilots may be wrecked on the homeward voyage, not by the unaided enchantments of the Witches, but by their working upon susceptible human souls. The great pilot Duncan will be wrecked as he comes homeward. Macbeth, tempted by the Witches, will wreck him, and the ship of state will drift upon the shoal. Macbeth himself will become the great pilot, to be wrecked by the Witches as he comes homeward. But he is wrecked, essentially, by the evil within him and his wife, which exposes them, and through them Scotland, to the evil enchantment. The Witches 'lead evil minds from evil to evil,' says Coleridge,[3] 'and have the power of tempting those who have been the tempters of themselves.' Macbeth's first words are:

> So foul and fair a day I have not seen.
>
> (I.iii.38)

Fair is foul, and foul is fair. Fair victory has bred foul thoughts, though the victory was a foul enough bloodbath to make such thoughts seem fair. Macbeth has destroyed Duncan's enemies at home and abroad. Should not the victor have the spoils? Macbeth has become what he fought; Duncan's enemy. Fair is foul. He dare not admit it, even to himself. Foul must show fair as yet. 'Shakespeare intimates by this,' says Dowden,[4] 'that although Macbeth has not yet set eyes upon these hags, the connection is already established between his soul and them. Their spells have already wrought upon his blood.'

THE WITCHES AFFECT MACBETH, BUT NOT BANQUO

Macbeth and Banquo see the Witches in the same moment. Macbeth is struck dumb by this shadowing forth of his own sinister and half-acknowledged thoughts. Foul as the Witches are they fascinate him. Banquo, his conscience untroubled, speaks at once and boldly, seeing foul as foul. The Witches will not speak to him at first. They are not powerful enough to tempt him. Banquo's words go whistling down the wind and the Witches stand ominously silent until Macbeth with difficulty gets out:

3. Samuel Taylor, in *Lectures and Notes on Shakespere* 4. Edward, in *A Critical Study of His Mind and Art*

> Speak if you can: what are you?
>
> (I.iii.47)

To him they answer, hailing him Glamis—Cawdor—King hereafter. (The Hail of the past, of the present, of the future, Dowden
observes.) At this last utterance Macbeth starts back in horror,
knowing from his own black thoughts how foul this seeming-
fair prediction is. Banquo, who has fought by his side all day and
never seen him blench, is amazed; but his incredulous cry,

> Good sir, why do you start; and seem to fear
> Things that do sound so fair?
>
> (I.iii.51–52)

strikes on deaf ears. Macbeth is in a trance of horror, half-
formed thoughts of murder rising from the depths of his
soul. What sounds fair to Banquo is foul to Macbeth, murder
most foul.

There is another moment of ominous silence, and then Banquo turns again upon the Witches. Their words have bewitched
Macbeth and he 'seems rapt withal.' What dare they speak to
him? They speak—but speak to Macbeth, although addressing
themselves to Banquo, appeal to Macbeth's jealousy as subtly as
they have just tempted his ambition. Macbeth's senses are violently restored by what he hears. Banquo's sons shall be kings,
though he be none! What can that mean? Already the weird sisters are disappearing into the gloom. For his very life he must
know more; whether or not Banquo hears it too he cannot
pause to consider. The opportunity may not come again:

> Stay, you imperfect speakers, tell me more. . . .
>   Say, from whence
> Upon this blasted heath you stop our way
> With such prophetic greeting?—Speak, I charge you.
>
> (I.iii.70–78)

But they are gone. Banquo is amazed, but no more. He made
no attempt to ask further questions of the Witches or hinder
their departure. Yet though they spoke to Banquo, Macbeth
cried, 'Tell me more,' and now they are gone he mutters anx-
iously, 'Would they had stayed!' Already his resolve is half-
made to throw in his lot with the instruments of darkness.
Banquo, whose soul is free, seeks to sever the strand woven
between Macbeth and the Witches. Perhaps, he says, it was
nothing but illusion after all:

> Were such things here, as we do speak about,
> Or have we eaten on the insane root,
> That takes the reason prisoner?
>
> (I.iii.83–85)

Macbeth makes short work of that. They have both the same recollection of what was said. Can two men have the same illusion in the same words at the same moment? He will not entertain the thought that he has been deceived. Macbeth believes in the Witches and is sorely troubled by the disparity between their prophecies to him and to his companion. His own evil thoughts already bind him to the Witches.

THE MESSENGERS SPUR MACBETH'S IMAGINATION FURTHER

Before they can say more, Ross and Angus enter. Our attention is focused on Macbeth's reception of their news, which we already know. The speeches of Ross and Angus in this scene are almost as though heard through Macbeth's ears. '*Macbeth* is remarkable beyond any other of Shakespeare's plays for the frequency and power of its tragic "irony,"' says A.W. Verity, and defines 'irony' as 'the difference between the facts as known to the audience and as imagined by the characters of the play or by some of them.' The double-meanings of the Witches' riddling prophecies have their counterpart in the undertones often momentarily audible in the speeches of many of the human characters. Scene two has had its share of this echoing and re-echoing undertone, as we shall see.

Macbeth's mind is still full of murderous thoughts against King Duncan and busy with the prophecy which seems to show that such a crime is preordained. Ross's first words are of the King's gratitude for Macbeth's victories, but before his heart can respond, he hears:

Thy personal venture in the rebels' fight,
His wonders and his praises do contend,
Which should be thine or his. Silenc'd with that. . . .

(I.iii.91–93)

Which should be thine or his, which Duncan's, which Macbeth's? In Macbeth's rebel heart that is the very question, and the answer is one that may well silence Duncan for ever. Dare Macbeth decide it for himself? At once Ross's words comment upon the thought:

Nothing afeared of what thyself didst make,
Strange images of death.

(I.iii.96–97)

Macbeth is not afraid to make strange images of death—must he now let conscience make a coward of him, and betray his own high destiny by being 'afeared'? Angus has taken up the tale for a moment:

> We are sent,
> To give thee from our royal master thanks;
> Only to herald thee into his sight,
> *Not pay thee.*
>
> (I.iii.100–103)

No! There is nothing that their royal master Duncan can give that would pay Macbeth for his day's work. Nothing . . . but his own royalty. Well may he stand in doubt which should be his and which Macbeth's! But Ross at once adds:

> And, for *an earnest of a greater honour,*
> He bade me, from him, call thee thane of Cawdor:
> In which addition, *hail,* most worthy thane.
>
> (I.iii.104–106)

The double blow is stupefying. 'Hail, most worthy thane' starts in his mind and ours the fateful echo:

> 1 *Witch:* All hail, Macbeth! hail to thee, thane of Glamis!
> 2 *Witch:* All hail, Macbeth! hail to thee, thane of Cawdor!
> 3 *Witch:* All hail, Macbeth! that shalt be king hereafter!
>
> (I.iii.48–50)

Now he has not only the instant confirmation of the prophecy that he will be thane of Cawdor, but he is given the title *'for an earnest of a greater honour'!* Ross has become an oracle, repeating the greatest promise of the Witches. (Ross is given no message from Duncan that would justify the promise of a greater honour! Shakespeare is careful to make it good in general terms in the following scene, but Ross's line has been written to play upon the prophecy, not simply to report the previous scene.)

Banquo's aside—'What! can the devil speak true?'—emphasizes that he has not hesitated in his hostility to the Witches, despite their fair promises to him; he is invulnerable to their temptations. Macbeth is only eager for confirmation of their infallibility. But he scarcely hears more than the first few words of Angus's answer about Cawdor's treachery. What Angus says has ominous meaning, too, if Macbeth would mark it. Duncan bade his messengers greet Macbeth as 'thane of Cawdor,' and they have just done so. Now Angus finishes with the news that the 'thane of Cawdor's'

> . . . *treason's capital,* confess'd and prov'd,
> *Have overthrown him.*
>
> (I.iii.115–16)

So, too, the new thane of Cawdor will be overthrown. Macbeth misses the omen. The 'earnest of a greater honour' still burns in his brain—

> Glamis, and thane of Cawdor!
The greatest is behind.
>
> (I.iii.116–17)

BANQUO SUSPECTS MACBETH'S THOUGHTS AND TRIES TO WARN HIM TO NO AVAIL

Now he feels Banquo's eyes fastened accusingly upon him. Why has Macbeth not greeted his new title with some exclamation to Ross and Angus about the prophecy which has just been made to him?—even if he thought it right to suppress the further prophecy that he should be king hereafter. He has said nothing in answer but the flat and forced, 'Thanks for your pains.' Now Macbeth mutters half-defiantly to Banquo, does he not hope his children shall be kings? Banquo's retort is unerring; he has read something of what is passing in Macbeth's mind and warns him against ambition for the crown.

> But 'tis strange:
> And oftentimes, to win us to our harm,
> The instruments of darkness tell us truths;
> Win us with honest trifles, to betray's
> In deepest consequence.
>
> (I.iii.122–26)

Macbeth will not be warned. He turns away from Banquo without a word, tragically quick to believe what he wishes to believe, whatever feeds ambition. The honest trifles, he tells himself, are but happy prologues to the imperial theme!

> This supernatural soliciting
> Cannot be ill;
>
> (I.iii.130–31)

But the thought runs straight to murder. Macbeth has willed the end but not yet the means. If this soliciting is good:

> why do I yield to that suggestion
> Whose horrid image doth unfix my hair,
> And make my seated heart knock at my ribs,
> Against the use of nature?
>
> (I.iii.134–37)

Yet Macbeth was 'Nothing afeard of what thyself didst *make*, Strange images of death.' The images of death that now strike his heart with unaccustomed fear, are strange, perhaps, only because they are not made but thought upon. To act against the use of nature might not be so dreadful after all: 'Present fears are less than horrible imaginings.' (I.iii.137-38)

His mind is still desperately seeking for a possible escape from the crime. As his wife contemptuously says, he would not play false and yet would wrongly win. 'He seems rapt withal,' (I.iii.57) Banquo had said when Macbeth first heard the Witches' prophesy, and now he says again, 'Look, how our partner's rapt.' (I.iii.142) The same evil thoughts have returned. For the moment the decision, as Coleridge says, is 'still in Macbeth's moral will.' He makes one last weak effort to break out of the spell by interpreting the prophecy fatalistically. If he is predestined to be King, chance may crown him without his stir. He need not take upon himself the burden of regicide. But as he says it he knows that if it is his fate to be King, it is his destiny to make his own way to the throne. Is he not man enough to throw off the consequences? When horrible imaginings have become present fears, present will soon become past:

> Come what come may,
> Time and the hour runs through the roughest day.
>
> (I.iii.146–47)

To his companions he says, after some belated compliments and thanks:

> Let us toward the King.

To dispel Banquo's suspicions he briefly promises 'at more time' (I.iii.152) they shall speak 'Our free hearts each to other.' The time will never come. Macbeth's heart is no longer free.

Macbeth Is All Middle

Stephen Booth

Stephen Booth argues that *Macbeth* is all middle because no element—events, factual knowledge, time, characters—has a clear beginning, ending, limit, or definition. He argues that the audience reacts to this limitless, nebulous quality by identifying with Macbeth and experiencing the play with him even though from an objective distance they would condemn him. Booth calls *Macbeth* a great tragedy because its limitlessness prompts the audience to experience terror along with the title character. Stephen Booth has taught English at the University of California at Berkeley. He has edited a collection of Shakespeare's sonnets and is the author of *An Essay on Shakespeare's Sonnets.*

It is easy enough to see that in the tragedies we value, the *imitation* (the play) is complete, has a beginning, a middle, and an end. That is not often true of the actions imitated; it is notably untrue in *Macbeth.*

It is true that *Macbeth* very definitely begins—more definitely than *King Lear* or *Othello* or *Hamlet,* which open on continuing situations. In *Macbeth* the witches come out and plan future action ("When shall we three meet again?") and promise an immediate relationship to the title character ("There to meet with Macbeth"—I.i.7). *Macbeth* also ends. Macduff enters with the head of Macbeth; everyone hails Malcolm king, and, in the last speech of the play, Malcolm ties off all the loose threads of Scottish politics. . . .

THE END HAS NO CLEAR END

On the other hand, it would also be true to say that *Macbeth* is all middle. For instance, the eminently final speech of Malcolm's is curiously reminiscent of Duncan's speeches when the earlier hurly-burly was done, when the earlier

Reprinted from Stephen Booth, *"King Lear," "Macbeth," Indefinition, and Tragedy* (New Haven: Yale University Press, 1983), by permission of the publisher. Copyright © 1983 by Yale University.

battle was lost and won. In Act I—with Macdonwald's head newly fixed upon the battlements in the midst of a battle that seems done and then picks up again—Duncan promised rewards and distributed titles. Specifically, Malcolm's distribution of earldoms and his general invitation to ceremonial journeying echo Duncan's gestures in I.iv.35–43. . . . Malcolm's "What's more to do / Which would be planted newly with the time" echoes Duncan's metaphor when he addresses Macbeth at their first (and only) onstage meeting: "I have begun to plant thee and will labor / To make thee full of growing." A vague, free-floating sense that the old cycle is starting over again in the new can also be evoked by the deluge of *Hail*'s that greets Malcolm's reign, as the witches hailed Macbeth's. Moreover, Malcolm's speech also denies its finality by introducing an audience that is six lines from the end of the play to new and doubtful information about Lady Macbeth, who has, for the last three scenes, been dead and done with in the audience's understanding.

The inconclusiveness coeval with the close of the action and the end of the play is—to the dismay of generations of actors and critics—actually demonstrated on the stage.

Macbeth speaks his last line, "Lay on, Macduff, / And damned be him that first cries, 'Hold, enough!'" (V.viii.33–34). The sentence asserts continuation. But its occasion bespeaks finality: Macbeth is trying "the last"; this is a fight to the death. The couplet rhyme bespeaks finality too. The immediately ensuing action is simultaneously complete (*Exeunt*—the scene is over) and incomplete (Macbeth and Macduff go off fighting, and we hear the fight continuing offstage). Then the completed scene continues. Macduff drives Macbeth right back out on the stage again and kills him. . . .

After Macbeth speaks what turns out to be his last line, the Folio stage direction say, *Exeunt fighting. Alarums. Enter Fighting, and Macbeth slaine.* The action called for by those directions tells an audience that Macbeth is dead—if only because there is no more plot left to be worked out. But the audience's knowledge is not neat, does not have comfortable handles on it, because Macbeth is not labeled as dead. The audience must itself maintain the equilibrium between the two realities while Macduff (or his director) manages to get the puffing corpse of Macbeth off the stage.

I have talked enough about the last moments of Macbeth the character and the last moments of *Macbeth* the play. By way of coda, however, let me point out that the nineteen-line interval between *Enter Fighting, and Macbeth slaine* and *Enter Macduffe; with Macbeths head* is largely taken up with an ostentatiously precise discussion of the state, location, and proper response to another corpse, that of young Siward:

ROSS. Your son, my lord, has paid a soldier's debt.
He only lived but till he was a man,
The which no sooner had his prowess confirmed
In the unshrinking station[1] where he fought
But like a man he died.
SIWARD.   Then he is dead?
ROSS. Ay, and brought off the field. Your cause of sorrow
Must not be measured by his worth, for then
It hath no end.
SIWARD.   Had he his hurts before?
ROSS. Ay, on the front.
SIWARD.   Why then, God's soldier be he.
[V.viii.39–47]

The dead Macbeth "hath no end"—at least no theatrically comfortable end. On the other hand, young Siward, who never strikes us as more than an incidental of the play, is put to rest with full expository rites. . . .

NOTHING SEEMS FINAL OR CONCLUSIVE

Finality is regularly unattainable throughout *Macbeth:* Macbeth and Lady Macbeth cannot get the murder of Duncan finished: Lady Macbeth has to go back with the knives. They cannot get done with Duncan himself: his blood will not wash off. Banquo refuses death in two ways: he comes back as a ghost, and (supposedly) he lives on in the line of Stuart kings into the actual present of the audience. The desirability and impossibility of conclusion is a regular concern of the characters, both in large matters ("The time has been / That, when the brains were out, the man would die, / And there an end"— (III.iv.78–80) and in such smaller ones as Macbeth's inability to achieve the temporary finality of sleep and Lady Macbeth's inability to cease her activity even in sleep itself. The concern for finality is incidentally present even in details like Macbeth's incapacity to pronounce "Amen."

What is true of endings is also true of beginnings. Lady Macbeth's mysteriously missing children present an ominous, unknown, but undeniable time before the beginning. Doubtful

---

1. **unshrinking station:** i.e., by standing firm and undismayed when he fought with Macbeth

beginnings are also incidentally inherent in such details of the play as Macduff's nonbirth. Indeed, the beginnings, sources, causes, of almost everything in the play are at best nebulous. . . .

The play, as play, has definition—a beginning, a middle, and an end—but its materials, even those that are used to designate its limits, provide insistent testimony to the artificiality, frailty, and ultimate impossibility of limits. A sense of limitlessness infuses every element of the play.

A good short example is the operation of limitless and directionless time in Macbeth's speech on the death of Lady Macbeth:

> She should have died hereafter:
> There would have been a time for such a word.
> To-morrow, and to-morrow, and to-morrow
> Creeps in this petty pace from day to day
> To the last syllable of recorded time,
> And all our yesterdays have lighted fools
> The way to dusty death. Out, out, brief candle!
> Life's but a walking shadow, a poor player
> That struts and frets his hour upon the stage
> And then is heard no more. It is a tale
> Told by an idiot, full of sound and fury,
> Signifying nothing.
>
> [V.v.17–28]

"Hereafter," which designates time future, here echoes time past in the play. It echoes Lady Macbeth's first words to Macbeth. In their first exchange, "by the all-hail hereafter" itself is an echo of the witches' prophecy of Macbeth's future ("All hail, Macbeth! that shalt be King hereafter"—I.iii.50), and it leads first into her lines on her sense of the future (even as she, who was not present when the witches spoke, is displaying knowledge of the past that she does not have) and then into a forecast of the immediate future, from which her death results and which is figured as a tomorrow that will never come:

> Great Glamis! worthy Cawdor!
> Greater than both, by the all-hail hereafter!
> Thy letters have transported me beyond
> This ignorant present, and I feel now
> The future in the instant.
> MACBETH.   My dearest love
> Duncan comes here to-night.
> LADY.   And when goes hence?
> MACBETH. To-morrow, as he purposes.
> LADY.   O, never
> Shall sun that morrow see!
>
> [I.v.52–59]

Tomorrow designates time future, but in the construction "Tomorrow, and tomorrow, and tomorrow" its plurality suggests its operation in the past, while the tense of the verb, *creeps*, is present. The direction in which it creeps should be

> **A CONCLUSION NEVER CONCLUDED**
>
> *Macbeth's act 1, scene 7 soliloquy occurs as the first event of the night of Duncan's murder. The speech is about his decision, but the lines within it do not stay fixed and the speech itself is never concluded.*

MACB. If it were done when 'tis done, then 'twere well
It were done quickly. If th' assassination
Could trammel[1] up the consequence, and catch,
With his surcease, success;[2] that but this blow
Might be the be-all and the end-all here,
But[3] here, upon this bank and shoal of time,
We'ld jump the life to come. But in these cases
We still have judgment here, that we but teach
Bloody instructions, which, being taught, return
To plague th' inventor. This even-handed justice
Commends th' ingredience of our poison'd chalice
To our own lips. He's here in double trust:
First, as I am his kinsman and his subject—
Strong both against the deed; then, as his host,
Who should against his murtherer shut the door,
Not bear the knife myself. Besides, this Duncan
Hath borne his faculties[4] so meek, hath been
So clear[5] in his great office, that his virtues
Will plead like angels, trumpet-tongu'd, against
The deep damnation of his taking-off;
And pity, like a naked new-born babe,[6]
Striding the blast, or heaven's cherubin, hors'd
Upon the sightless couriers[7] of the air,
Shall blow the horrid deed in every eye,
That tears shall drown the wind. I have no spur
To prick the sides of my intent, but only
Vaulting ambition, which o'erleaps itself
And falls on th' other side.

[*Enter* LADY MACBETH.]

How now? What news?

1. **trammel:** to entangle in a net 2. **With ... success:** i.e., if only the murder could have no after effects but be final and successful at Duncan's death (surcease) 3. **But:** even 4. **faculties:** powers 5. **clear:** innocent 6. **naked ... babe:** i.e., an object which moves the hardhearted to pity 7. **sightless couriers:** unseen messengers

future, but the ultimate future is described in words ("last," "recorded") that suit and suggest the ultimate past. The next clause is actually in the past tense. The journey of yesterdays becomes undistinguishable from that of tomorrows, and time past fuses with time future. "Out, out," the candle, and the walking shadow in the next lines suggest Lady Macbeth in the sleepwalking scene and thus, in a sense, introduce her alive into a speech of which her death is the occasion but of which she seemed no longer to be the subject. Nothing in the play or in the speech is finished for good. . . .

CHARACTERS LACK LIMITS

What is true of words, sentences, and speeches is also true of the characters in *Macbeth;* they will not stay within limits either. Take, for example, the witches—the first characters we apprehend and the first characters the play tells us we comprehend. They intend to "meet with Macbeth." Are they his accomplices or his enemies? The play behaves as if that were immediately obvious to us, but it is not. We are also ignorant of their relation to the action: do they foresee events or ordain them? Banquo encapsulates the issue and—in the manner by which the whole play takes us through and beyond the doubts it contains—overwhelms the problem in a syntax that casually fuses the alternatives:

> If you can look into the seeds of time
> And say which grain will grow and which will not,
> Speak then to me, who neither beg nor fear
> Your favors nor your hate.

[I.iii.58–63]

Among the many other things we do not finally know is whether the witches are natural or supernatural. If natural, are they male or are they female? The actors Shakespeare's audience saw were male, but what about the three bearded sisters those men played? They are indisputably female, but the play insists that we momentarily pursue the issue before returning to the facts already obvious from the repetition of the word *sister* and manifest in the pronoun *her* even at the moment of gratuitous, theatrically complicated doubt:

> You seem to understand me,
> By each at once her choppy finger laying
> Upon her skinny lips. You should be women,
> And yet your beards forbid me to interpret
> That you are so.

[I.iii .43–47]

And, if the witches are not natural, are they real or imaginary? Where in the spectrum of unnatural evidences do they belong? . . .

What matters here is not hunting down an answer to the question "What are the witches?" All the critical and theatrical efforts to answer that question demonstrate that the question cannot be answered. What those frantic answers also demonstrate—and what matters—is the fact of the question. The play does not require that it be answered. Thinking about the play's action does. As we watch the play, the witches have definition, but we cannot afterward say what that definition is. As we watch the play, we know what we cannot know; we possess knowledge that remains unattainable. That kind of paradoxical capacity is, I think, what the play gives us that makes us call it great.

The greatness of *Macbeth*, I think, derives from Shakespeare's ability to minimize neither our sense of limitlessness nor our sense of the constant and comforting limitation of artistic pattern, order, and coherence. . . .

THE AUDIENCE IDENTIFIES WITH MACBETH

I submit that the tragedy of the play *Macbeth* is not of the character Macbeth and that it does not happen on the stage. The tragedy occurs in the audience, in miniature in each little failure of categories and at its largest in the failure of active moral categories to hold the actions and actors proper to them. An audience undergoes its greatest tragedy in joining its mind to Macbeth's both in his sensitive awareness of evil and his practice of it. Like Macbeth, it knows evil but, even in the last two acts when Malcolm is repeatedly preferred as the wholesome substitute for Macbeth, it persists in seeing the play through Macbeth's eyes. The audience itself cannot keep itself in the category dictated by its own morality, even though its moral judgments of characters and their actions are dictated entirely by that morality. . . .

Because *Macbeth* evokes conflicting responses that could but do not collide in our consciousnesses, and because it both includes and omits to exploit logical inconsistencies in its characters' behavior, the experience of seeing or reading *Macbeth* is experience of an object that is under constant pressure from within—an object full of volatile elements always ready to meet and explode. . . .

TRAGEDY PERMITS THE EXPERIENCE OF TERROR

The events depicted in *Macbeth* are not complete, not a closed unit with a beginning, a middle, and an end. Similarly, an audience's experience of *Macbeth* is of truth beyond the limits of categories. That experience, which I think is what we are labeling when we use the word *tragedy* is made bearable by a vehicle, the fabric of the play, which has limits, has pattern, and is insistently man-made. . . .

What *Macbeth* does for us—what successful dramatic tragedy does for us—is like what the word *tragedy* does for real-life tragedies: it gives local habitation and a name to the most terrifying of things, "a deed without a name" (IV.i.49), without denying its namelessness, its incomprehensibility, its indefinition.

The Facets of Macbeth's Imagination

Gareth Lloyd Evans

Gareth Lloyd Evans claims that Macbeth suffers because he has such an active imagination, which leads him to be filled with personal guilt and to alienate him from his wife. Evans, however, also portrays Macbeth as a man capable of action, an ability that becomes his only resource for gaining authority and control over his imagination and his situation. Gareth Lloyd Evans teaches dramatic literature at the University of Birmingham in England and is a drama critic for the *Guardian* and other journals. He is the author of a five-volume guide to Shakespeare's plays and *J.B. Priestley, Dramatist.*

Macbeth is cursed by imagination. He can perform no deed without testing its uttermost consequences. His wish that 'this blow might be the be all and the end all here' is, considering his mental make-up, terribly ironic. The mere brute man commits murder with immediate access of physical violence, having no imagination to project motive or consequence either backwards or forwards in time. But Macbeth is saddled with the frightening ability both to remember and to foresee in images of engulfing power—in a man of action set upon a course of treacherous murder, this is a curse. In his soliloquy spoken before Duncan's chamber, his imagination can be seen working in phase with the present-tense action of the deed—the real dagger he is about to use being also a dagger suspended in the chambers of his own mind. The real steps he is taking must be unheard, otherwise they might 'prate' of his intentions. Yet as soon as he returns from the chamber his imagination begins to work in the past tense, he remembers a noise he heard; he recalls that one laughed in his sleep, the other cried 'murder', then 'God

Excerpted from Gareth Lloyd Evans, *The Upstart Crow: An Introduction to Shakespeare's Plays*, edited and revised by Barbara Lloyd Evans (London: J.M. Dent, 1982). Reprinted by permission of Orion Publishing.

bless us', then 'Amen'. His memory pushes inwards upon him, like mounting waves, knocking his words into a growing rhythm of imagined guilt:

> 'Still it cried "Sleep no more" to all the house;
> Glamis hath murder'd sleep; and therefore Cawdor
> Shall sleep no more—Macbeth shall sleep no more.'
>
> (II.2.41–3)

However, the fact that this man of action has omitted an elementary precaution—to bring back the daggers from the murder chamber—is surely a measure of the extent to which his ranging imagination has accompanied and fractured the simple performance of the deed. At this point, two considerations enter into the critical estimation of Macbeth's state.

The first concerns his realization of his guilt. To what extent, indeed, at this stage, has Macbeth a conscience? To the extent that conscience implies regret at a deed committed which is subsequently wished uncommitted, he has a large one. In the murder scene his huge imagination frightens his conscience into activity, and the implications of the images it conjures up—the voice saying that he shall sleep no more, his bloody hands—eventually come to mean one thing:

> 'Wake Duncan with thy knocking! I would thou couldst.'
>
> (II.2.73)

Yet, at this point, Macbeth does not have the kind of conscience which shows any pity for the victim of a deed committed. Indeed, far from regret over killing Duncan, the implication is that the real regret he feels is for himself and what the deed's implications have in store for him—moral conpunctions have been replaced by self-indulgent imagination.

LADY MACBETH'S LESSER IMAGINATION

The second important matter of interpretation concerns the nature of the relationship between Macbeth and his wife. It is customary to imagine them and, indeed, to depict them, as a closely-knit 'fiend-like' duo. . . .

Later, we see them together, and in the banquet scene she performs an act of tremendous will in holding together (if only just) her shattered husband. Yet it is at the point of the murder when they are 'but young in deed' that, paradoxically, these two begin to draw away from one another, or rather, Macbeth draws himself away from his wife. [Critic] George Hunter writes: 'The deed itself is a denial of all social obligations, all sharing, all community of feeling even

with his wife.' But the separation has another element in it
as well for where drawing away from Lady Macbeth is concerned, the simple fact is that she cannot follow him into the
regions to which his imagination is taking him. As his imagination weaves around the words 'Amen', 'God bless us' and
'sleep', pushing him into the final horror of:

> 'Will all great Neptune's ocean wash this blood
> Clean from my hand?'
>
> (II.2.60)

her responses are remarkably banal. 'Consider it not so
deeply'. 'What do you mean?' and she reveals her profound
imaginative insensitivity when she says:

> '. . . The sleeping and the dead
> Are but as pictures; 'tis the eye of childhood
> That fears a painted devil. If he do bleed,
> I'll guild the faces of the grooms withal,
> For it must seem their guilt.'
>
> (II.2. 53-57)

And there can be no doubt about her inability to follow Macbeth in his journey through hells of his own making, after
her remark that:

> '. . . retire we to our chamber:
> A little water clears us of this deed.'
>
> (II.2.66–7)

—in itself an ironic reversal of Macbeth's belief that his hand
will turn all the ocean to red.

MACBETH IS ISOLATED FROM SOCIETY AND INDIVIDUALS

Macbeth, then, becomes isolated from society because of the
murder, and isolated from individuals, even the closest to
him, because of the far greater imaginative power he has. . . .

The loneliness, however, which cloaks him at the death of
Duncan gives him also, paradoxically, a new kind of
strength. The Macbeth we see after Macduff has arrived to
wake Duncan is not the tortured man of the previous scene.
There is an icy kind of calm about him. In reply to questions
and remarks, he is terse, as if screwing his courage for a
posture of strength. 'Good morrow both'. 'Not yet'. 'I'll bring
you to him'. ''Twas a rough night'. He keeps his head while
the discovery of the murder creates its own chaos and, in the
end, takes charge of the situation:

> 'Let's briefly put on manly readiness
> And meet i' th'hall together.'
>
> (II.3.133–4)

His calm is the more remarkable in the face of the atmosphere of suspicion which the murder of the grooms has created, for in this and the following scene, Shakespeare, by hints and innuendoes, gives us a faint but ineradicable sense that Macbeth's action has not passed without whispers of suspicion. . . .

The seeds of suspicion in Macduff's mind are germinated when he leaves for Fife, and Banquo's reaction, III.1 is:

'Thou hast it now—King, Cawdor, Glamis, all
As the weird women promis'd; and I fear
Thou play'd most foully for't;'

(III.1.1–3)

Suspicion, disorder, have come to the surface. Where now does Macbeth stand?

First, his isolation is virtually complete; second, his acquisition of the throne has, from the very beginning, been attended by disorder, suspicion and a perplexed mind for himself and his queen. However, as long as Macbeth can remain active, can at least give himself the illusion that he has some control over his destiny, he seems decisive, authoritative, and unswamped by imagination. . . .

The extent to which the acquisition of kingship gives Macbeth a quality of decision is seldom noted by critics, nor is it always communicated by actors. It makes itself quite manifest in Act III.2 when Lady Macbeth enters and asks him why he keeps himself so much to himself. The answer she receives is clear-headed, rational. He knows exactly the position he is in, and knows, equally exactly, what his next step will be: 'Let your remembrance apply to Banquo.' Just as significant as this access of authority and rationality is a pronounced shift in the way in which his imagination works as he moves from a state when it controls him, to a state when he seems able to call upon it, exults in its power, making it do what he asks. It is as if the fulfilment of his ambition (though it has cost him much) has strengthened the man, and there is irony in the fact that his rationality, control, and authority suggest that, were all the circumstances different, he would have been an efficient and respected monarch. This possibility is the more distinct when we see him at the beginning of the banquet scene, when he is completely in command gracious and regal:

'Our self will mingle with society
And play the humble host.'

(III.4.3–4)

THE STRUGGLE BETWEEN THE FORMER MACBETH AND THE NEW

The 'fit' which comes upon him with the appearance of Banquo's ghost is, in effect, a struggle between the 'new' rational Macbeth, and the former weak, indecisive man, cursed by imagination. The rhythmic movement of the scene is superbly controlled by Shakespeare. The first wave knocks Macbeth out of sense:

> 'Thou canst not say I did it; never shake
> Thy gory locks at me.'

(III.4.50-1)

The second wave plunges his mind into a cauldron of uncontrollable images:

> 'If charnel-houses and our graves must send
> Those that we bury back, our monuments
> Shall be the maw of kites.'

(III.4.71-3)

The third wave sucks all away, leaving him shattered but momentarily restored to equilibrium:

> 'I do forget:
> Do not muse at me, my most worthy friends;'

(III.4.84-5)

With the return of the ghost comes the fourth wave, which causes his anguished mind to try and will this horrible image into a shape and a situation which he can control:

> 'Approach thou like the rugged Russian bear,
> The arm'd rhinoceros, or th'Hyrcan tiger;
> Take any shape but that, and my firm nerves
> Shall never tremble.'

(III.4.100-3)

The fifth wave is a return of the third—imagination overpowers him; exhausted as he is, neither authority, will nor reason can hold back the monstrous images:

> 'You make me strange
> Even to the disposition that I owe,'

(III.4.112-3)

Finally, when all have left, this battered man returns to some semblance of order within himself. He grasps again at the one thing which is indigenous to him, which gives him equilibrium and rationality—the possibility of action:

> 'Strange things I have in head that will to hand,
> Which must be acted ere they may be scann'd'

(III.4.139-40)

These two lines sum up Macbeth's personality. He is of that kind whose disposition is to act and then to speculate. His tragedy is that his weak moral fibre, in combination with his powerful imagination, confounds his will to control himself in acting 'rightly' or 'wrongly'. . . .

MACBETH'S IMAGINATION PERFORMS ITS LAST TASK AND DIES

The death of his wife enables him to put his imagination to its final task—to assess the meaning of existence. Having done this, imagination itself dies—there is nothing more it can do since even its prophetic powers add up to nothing:

> 'Life's but a walking shadow, a poor player,
> That struts and frets his hour upon the stage,
> And then is heard no more; it is a tale
> Told by an idiot, full of sound and fury,
> Signifying nothing.'

(V.5.24–8)

So, with fear gone, imagination dispossessed, Macbeth is left with that one quality which, without ambition, without imagination, without moral weakness, might well have made him a man of greatness—the will to act. One by one the witches' equivocating prophecies are revealed for what they are, but at each withdrawal of illusory safety, Macbeth makes renewed decisions to act:

> 'At least we'll die with harness on our back.'

(V.5.52)

> 'But bear-like I must fight the course.'

(V.7.2)

> 'Yet I will try the last. Before my body
> I throw my warlike shield. Lay on, Macduff;
> And damm'd be him, that first cries, "Hold, enough!"'

(V.8.32–4)

Macbeth is often relegated to the status of 'unsympathetic' tragic villain. His stark and violent butchery contrasts with Hamlet's wavering, Othello's misguided pride, Lear's foolishness, as having no excuse with which to command any kind of admiration or pity from reader or audience. Yet, if we place him alongside Iago, who *seems* equally blandly and totally evil, can we in the final analysis relegate him to a role of total infamy? Throughout the whole play of *Macbeth*, but most notably in the early acts, there is a sense created that here is a man who could, most positively, be good and great and what we witness is a tragedy of the most painful, and yet pure kind—that of a man in whose personality there is a dissociation between certain characteristics which, in themselves, are potentially admirable. He has a will for action, a powerful imagination, self-knowledge, an ability to distinguish between good and evil, a strong awareness of love, fidelity and honour. As they are mixed in this play, what emerges is evil; but in the inevitability with which he surrounds himself with evil, and in the searing self-knowledge which accompanies it, Macbeth becomes a suffering man. . . .

In the end, however, all the characters pale into insignificance in comparison with Macbeth himself and the curious fact is that whatever moral judgements one makes on him, whatever allowance of sympathy one is prepared to grant or to withhold, he cannot be forced out of one's imagination. As [critic John] Kemble noted: 'In the performance on the stage, the valour of the tyrant, hateful as he is, invariably commands the admiration of every spectator of the play.' Shakespeare's theatrical power in fact can exert such a fascination on us that it can weaken any disposition we have to question intellectually the moral pattern of the play. Chaos is expunged in the end, order reasserts itself, the commonwealth, tested sorely by evil, is brought back to health. Yet it is not this that we remember when we leave the book or the performance. We remember only that we have experienced (in [critic] John Wain's words): '. . . not so much with our visual imagination as with our hands, teeth, throats, our very skin, hair and nails, a terrifying reality.'

Chronology

1557

Shakespeare's parents, John Shakespeare and Mary Arden, marry

1558

Elizabeth I becomes queen of England

1561

Philosopher and statesman Francis Bacon born; advanced as actual writer of Shakespeare's plays by skeptics in modern age

1562

First English participation in New World slave trade from Africa

1564

William Shakespeare born; English dramatist Christopher Marlowe born; Italian painter, sculptor, and architect Michelangelo dies at eighty-eight

1569

John Shakespeare becomes bailiff of Stratford

CA. 1570

Emilia Bassano, daughter of a court musician and suggested real-life dark lady of the Sonnets, born

1572

Ben Jonson, English playwright and poet, born

1576

The Theatre, England's first playhouse, is built in London

1577–1580

Sir Francis Drake's first English voyage around the world

1578

Historian and printer Raphael Holinshed publishes *Chronicles of English History to 1575*, source of material for Shakespeare's histories

1582

Shakespeare marries Anne Hathaway

1583

Daughter Susanna born

1584

Sir Walter Raleigh founds Virginia colony on Roanoke Island

1585

Twins Hamnet and Judith born

1587

Execution of Mary, Queen of Scots, by order of Elizabeth I; Marlowe's *Tamburlaine* performed in London

1587–1590

Shakespeare acting and touring

1588

Spanish Armada defeated by British navy, making way for England's ascendancy in world trade and colonization

1591

1 Henry VI

1591–1592

2 and *3 Henry VI*

1592

Plague in London causes closure of theaters; Robert Greene attacks Shakespeare in print, the first known reference to Shakespeare's reputation or work; Galileo proves objects fall at the same rate regardless of their weight, in Pisa

1592–1593

The Comedy of Errors; Sonnets; *Richard III*

1593

Plague in London continues; Marlowe dies in tavern brawl; *Titus Andronicus; The Taming of the Shrew; The Two Gentlemen of Verona; Love's Labour's Lost; Venus and Adonis* published

1594

Lord Chamberlain's Men, Shakespeare's acting company, formed; *The Rape of Lucrece* published

1594–1595

A Midsummer Night's Dream; Romeo and Juliet; Richard II

1595–1596

The Merchant of Venice

1596

Shakespeare applies for and receives coat of arms in his father's name, achieves gentleman status; Hamnet Shakespeare dies; *King John*

1597

Shakespeare buys New Place, property in Stratford that becomes his family's home; *1 Henry IV*

1598

The Theatre torn down, timbers used for new Globe; *2 Henry IV; Much Ado About Nothing*

1599

Globe theater opens; *Henry V; As You Like It; Julius Caesar; The Merry Wives of Windsor;* "The Passionate Pilgrim" published

1600–1601

Twelfth Night; Hamlet; Troilus and Cressida

1601

John Shakespeare dies; "The Phoenix and the Turtle"

1602

Shakespeare buys land at Stratford; *Othello*

1603

Bubonic plague strikes London; Elizabeth I dies; James I becomes king of England; English conquest of Ireland; Lord Chamberlain's Men become King's Men; *All's Well That Ends Well*

1604

Measure for Measure

1605

Repression of Catholics and Puritans; Gunpowder Plot to kill James I and members of Parliament; Shakespeare invests in

Stratford tithes; world's first newspaper begins publication in Antwerp

1606

Visit by the king of Denmark; Ben Jonson's *Volpone; King Lear; Macbeth*

1607

Jamestown, Virginia, founded; daughter Susanna marries Dr. John Hall

1607–1609

Antony and Cleopatra; Coriolanus; Timon of Athens (unfinished); *Pericles*

1608

Plague in London; King's Men acquire Blackfriars theater; granddaughter Elizabeth Hall born; Mary Arden Shakespeare dies

1609

Sonnets and "A Lover's Complaint" published by Thomas Thorpe, an edition believed unauthorized; Johannes Kepler proves planetary orbits are elliptical

1610

Cymbeline

1610–1611

The Winter's Tale

1611

The Maydenhead of the first musicke that ever was printed for the Virginalls, first book of keyboard music in England; King James Bible published; Shakespeare contributes to highway bill, repairing roads between Stratford and London; *The Tempest*

1612

Shakespeare's brother Gilbert dies

1612–1613

Henry VIII

1613

The Globe burns down; Shakespeare's brother Richard dies; Shakespeare buys house in Blackfriars area; Galileo says Copernicus was right

1615

Miguel de Cervantes completes *Don Quixote* in Spain

1616

Daughter Judith marries Thomas Quiney; Shakespeare dies; Vatican arrests Galileo

1623

Anne Hathaway Shakespeare dies; actors Condell and Heminge publish Shakespeare's collected plays in a single volume known as the First Folio

FOR FURTHER RESEARCH

ABOUT WILLIAM SHAKESPEARE AND *MACBETH*

Peter Alexander, *Shakespeare's Life and Art.* London: James Nisbet, 1939.

A.C. Bradley, *Shakespearean Tragedy: Lectures on* Hamlet, Othello, King Lear, Macbeth. London: Macmillan, 1960.

John C. Bromley, *The Shakespearean Kings.* Boulder: Colorado Associated University Press, 1971.

Ivor Brown, *How Shakespeare Spent the Day.* New York: Hill and Wang, 1963.

Victor L. Cahn, *Shakespeare the Playwright: A Companion to the Complete Tragedies, Histories, Comedies, and Romances.* London: Praeger, 1996.

Lily B. Campbell, *Shakespeare's Tragic Heroes: Slaves of Passion.* Gloucester, MA: Peter Smith, 1973

E.K. Chambers, *Shakespeare: A Survey.* New York: Hill and Wang, 1958.

S.T. Coleridge, *Shakespearean Criticism* (1811–1834), ed. T.M. Raysor. Cambridge, MA: Harvard University Press, 1930.

Hardin Craig and David Berington, *An Introduction to Shakespeare.* Rev. ed. Glenview, IL: Scott, Foresman, 1975.

Edward Dowden, *Shakespeare: A Critical Study of His Mind and Art.* New York: Harper & Brothers, 1880.

Gareth and Barbara Lloyd Evans, *The Shakespeare Companion.* New York: Charles Scribner's Sons, 1978.

Levi Fox, *The Shakespeare Handbook.* Boston: G.K. Hall, 1987.

Roland Mushat Frye, *Shakespeare's Life and Times: A Pictorial Record.* Princeton, NJ: Princeton University Press, 1967.

Harley Granville-Barker and G.B. Harrison, eds., *A Companion to Shakespeare Studies.* New York: Cambridge University Press, 1934.

Alice Griffin, ed., *The Sources of Ten Shakespearean Plays.* New York: Thomas Y. Crowell, 1966.

F.E. Halliday, *Shakespeare and His Critics.* New York: Schocken Books, 1963.

Alfred Harbage, ed., *Shakespeare: The Tragedies: A Collection of Critical Essays,* Englewood Cliffs, NJ: Prentice-Hall, 1964.

G.B. Harrison. *Shakespeare's Tragedies.* London: Routledge and Kegan Paul, 1951.

Dennis Kay, *Shakespeare: His Life, Work, and Era.* New York: William Morrow, 1992.

Victor Kiernan, *Shakespeare: Poet and Citizen.* New York: Verso, 1993.

Sidney Lee, *A Life of William Shakespeare.* New York: Dover, 1968.

E.F.C. Ludowyk, *Understanding Shakespeare.* Cambridge, England: Cambridge University Press, 1964.

Dieter Mehl, *Shakespeare's Tragedies: An Introduction.* New York: Cambridge University Press, 1983.

John Middleton Murry, *Shakespeare.* New York: Harcourt, Brace, 1936.

Richard G. Moulton, *Shakespeare as a Dramatic Artist: A Popular Illustration of the Principles of Scientific Criticism.* New York: Dover, 1966.

Charles Norman, *The Playmaker of Avon.* Philadelphia: David McKay, 1949.

Dorothy Ogburn and Charlton Ogburn Jr., *Shake-speare: The Man Behind the Name.* New York: William Morrow, 1962.

H.M. Richmond, *Shakespeare's Political Plays.* Gloucester, MA: Peter Smith, 1967.

A.L. Rowse, *Shakespeare the Man.* New York: Harper & Row, 1973.

———, *What Shakespeare Read and Thought.* New York: Coward, McCall & Geoghagan, 1981.

A.L. Rowse and John Hedgecoe, *Shakespeare's Land: A Journey Through the Landscape of Elizabethan England.* San Francisco: Chronicle Books, 1987.

S. Schoenbaum, *William Shakespeare: A Documentary Life.* New York: Oxford University Press in association with The Scholar Press, 1975.

Lloyd Sears, *Shakespeare's Philosophy of Evil.* North Quincy, MA: Christopher, 1974.

Edith Sitwell, *A Notebook on William Shakespeare.* Boston: Beacon Press, 1948.

Robert Speaight, *Nature in Shakespearean Tragedy.* London: Hollis & Carter, 1955.

Theodore Spencer, *Shakespeare and the Nature of Man: Lowell Lectures, 1942.* 2nd ed. London: Collier-Macmillan, 1949.

D.A. Traversi, *An Approach to Shakespeare: From* Troilus and Cressida *to* The Tempest. Vol. 2. Garden City, NY: Doubleday, 1969.

Stanley Wells, ed., *The Cambridge Companion to Shakespeare Studies.* London: Cambridge University Press, 1986.

ABOUT ELIZABETHAN THEATERS AND ENGLISH HISTORY

Joseph Quincy Adams, *Shakespearean Playhouses.* New York: Houghton Mifflin, 1917.

Maurice Ashley, *Great Britain to 1688.* Ann Arbor: University of Michigan Press, 1961.

Arthur Bryant, *Spirit of England.* London: William Collins, 1982.

Elizabeth Burton, *The Pageant of Elizabethan England.* New York: Charles Scribner's Sons, 1958.

Will and Ariel Durant, *The Age of Reason Begins: A History of European Civilization in the Period of Shakespeare, Bacon, Montaign, Rembrandt, Galileo, and Descartes: 1558–1658.* Vol. 7 of *The Story of Civilization.* New York: Simon and Schuster, 1961.

Alfred Harbage, *Shakespeare's Audience.* New York: Columbia University Press, 1941.

G.B. Harrison, *Elizabethan Plays and Players.* Ann Arbor: University of Michigan Press, 1956.

A.V. Judges, *The Elizabethan Underworld.* New York: Octagon Books, 1965.

Walter Raleigh, ed., *Shakespeare's England.* 2 vols. Oxford: Clarendon Press, 1916.

Shakespeare and the Theatre. London: Members of the Shakespeare Association of London, 1927. (A series of papers by a variety of critics.)

E.M.W. Tillyard, *The Elizabethan World Picture.* New York: Macmillan, 1943.

George Macaulay Trevelyan, *The Age of Shakespeare and the Stuart Period.* Vol. 2 of *Illustrated English Social History.* London: Longmans, Green, 1950.

ORGANIZATIONS TO CONTACT

The following Shakespeare societies have information or publications available to interested readers. Descriptions of the organizations are derived from materials provided by the societies themselves. This list was compiled upon the date of publication. Names and phone numbers are subject to change.

International Shakespeare Association (ISA)
The Shakespeare Center
Henley St.
Stratford-upon-Avon, Warwickshire, England
CV37 6 QW
phone: 44 1789 204016
fax: 44 1789 296083

The association gathers and disseminates information on Shakespearean research, publications, translations, and performances. It maintains and circulates a diary of future performances, conferences, opportunities for graduate work, and educational experiments relating to Shakespeare's works. Its publications include *Congress Proceedings,* a record of the quinquennial World Shakespeare Congress, next held in 2001.

Shakespeare Assocation of America (SAA)
Southern Methodist University
Department of English
Dallas, TX 75275
Nancy Elizabeth Hodge, Executive Director

The association provides members with an opportunity to discuss Shakespeare's life, plays, poems, and influence. Through development or continuation of appropriate projects, the association seeks to advance research, criticism, teaching, and production of Shakespearean and other Renaissance drama. It conducts seminars, workshops, and lectures; maintains a mailing list; publishes a semiannual bulletin; and sponsors the annual World Shakespeare Congress.

Shakespeare Data Bank (SDB)
1217 Ashland Ave.
Evanston, IL 60202
Louis Marder, Editor and CEO
phone: (708) 475-7550
fax: (708) 475-2415

The database compiles past scholarship and updated materials on the biographical, bibliographical, pedagogical, educational, glossorial, textual, scholarly, critical, interpretative, literary, theatrical, authorship, artistic, illustrative, thematic, statistical, historical, and related aspects of Shakespeare and his works. Members maintain the Shakespeare Hall of Fame and museum.

Shakespeare Oxford Society (SOS)
Greenridge Pk.
7D Taggart Dr.
Nashua, NH 03060-5591
Leonard Deming, Membership Chairman
phone: (603) 888-1453 or (508) 349-2087
e-mail: business@shakespeare.oxford.im.com

The society provides research material, including books, periodicals, artwork, and archival text, on the history of the Elizabethan period of English literature. It explores and attempts to verify evidence bearing on the authorship of works attributed to Shakespeare, particularly evidence indicating that Edward de Vere, the seventeenth earl of Oxford, was the true author, and searches for original manuscripts in England to support its theories. It conducts research and educational programs and maintains a speakers' bureau. It publishes the quarterly *Shakespeare Oxford Society Newsletter* and sponsors an annual fall conference.

WORKS BY WILLIAM SHAKESPEARE

Editor's Note: Many of the dates on this list are approximate. Because manuscripts identified with the date of writing do not exist, scholars have determined the most accurate available date, either of the writing or of the first production of each play.

1 Henry VI (1591)

2 and *3 Henry VI* (1591–1592)

The Comedy of Errors; Richard III; Sonnets (1592–1593)

Titus Andronicus; The Taming of the Shrew; The Two Gentlemen of Verona; Love's Labour's Lost; publication of *Venus and Adonis* (1593)

Publication of *The Rape of Lucrece* (1594)

A Midsummer Night's Dream; Romeo and Juliet; Richard II (1594–1595)

The Merchant of Venice (1595–1596)

King John (1596)

1 Henry IV (1597)

2 Henry IV; Much Ado About Nothing (1598)

Henry V; As You Like It; Julius Caesar; The Merry Wives of Windsor; publication of "The Passionate Pilgrim" (1599)

Twelfth Night; Hamlet; Troilus and Cressida (1600–1601)

"The Phoenix and the Turtle" (1601)

Othello (1602)

All's Well That Ends Well (1603)

Measure for Measure (1604)

King Lear; Macbeth (1606)

Antony and Cleopatra; Coriolanus; Timon of Athens (unfinished); *Pericles* (1607–1609)

Sonnets and "A Lover's Complaint" first published by Thomas Thorpe (1609)

Cymbeline (1610)

The Winter's Tale (1610–1611)

The Tempest (1611)

Henry VIII (1612–1613)

INDEX